Fathering Children with Disabilities

Geert Van Hove

Fathering Children with Disabilities

New Perspectives on Disability Studies and Family Care

palgrave
macmillan

Geert Van Hove
Special Needs Education
Ghent University
Ghent, Belgium

ISBN 978-3-031-82854-6 ISBN 978-3-031-82960-4 (eBook)
https://doi.org/10.1007/978-3-031-82960-4

This Palgrave Macmillan imprint is published by the registered company Springer Nature Switzerland AG.
The registered company address is: Gewerbestrasse 11, 6330 Cham, Switzerland

From: …. It is the mother who 'produces' the infant, it is she who 'gives' it birth. If 'the product' turns out to be defective, the mother is likely to perceive this as a defect in something she has labored to produce…. (Smith & Neisworth, 1975, in: Ferguson et al., 2020)

Over: … The most important thing that happens when a child with disabilities is born is that a child is born. The most important thing that happens when a couple becomes parents of a child with disabilities is that a couple becomes parents… (Ferguson & Ash, 1989, 108)

To: …. Is there any place within the society where inclusion already exist, full-blown? And the answer is: yes! It exists within a lot of families…. (Douglas Biklen in: Including Samuel, documentary of film maker Dan Habib)

Preface

When I told people that I was preparing a booklet on fathers of children with disabilities, some of them raised their eyebrows. These are the friends and colleagues who quickly refer to the (extensive) sociological research that has been done for years on the division of labor in families.

I knew the trends, didn't I? One very influential piece of research talked about 'the second shift' (Hochschild & Machung, 1989) to show that if women were already working outside the home, when they came home, they were working much more (the second shift) than their partners were. Yes, I knew what the trends were.

Indeed, I know that despite changing perceptions about gender, work, and domestic tasks, several researchers (see e.g. Glorieux et al., 2015; Audenaert, 2023) seem to come to the same conclusions: despite increasingly involved fathers, and despite the increase in families where both partners work from home, and despite policies that should allow for a more balanced division of labor, and despite changing perceptions (especially among the highly educated), statistics show that women even if they have a job in society still spend much more time—the studies we refer to for Flanders speak of twice or at least one and a half times as much time—on housework and childcare than men. It is striking that these trends appear to be similar over time (see Bianchi et al., 2000) and across countries (see Craigh & Mullan, 2011 for international comparisons).

In fact, the conclusion is: 'Fathers have started to contribute slightly more to childcare and domestic work, but the distribution remains unequal…' (Audenaert, 2023).

And yet. I was looking for the father's perspective.

When I told people that I was preparing a booklet on fathers of children with disabilities, some others also raised their eyebrows. These are the friends and colleagues who quickly refer to the (extensive) psychopathological research that has been done for years on families with children with disabilities.

Many psychopathological studies have been conducted on fathers and mothers raising children with disabilities. More recent studies have also focused very specifically on the (mental) health of the fathers (no longer as a comparison for the situation of the mothers) and also on their (un) healthy lifestyle. A more recent study in the context of Bourke-Taylor et al. (2021) used a number of online questionnaires and a few open-ended questions to address the fathers in their study. The three instruments used—the Depression Anxiety Stress Scale (DASS), the Health Promoting Activities Scale (HPAS-M), and the Fathers of Children with Developmental Challenges (FCDC) scale—already say a lot about the hypotheses from which they started. The latter scale was developed '…to assess fathers' perceptions of the supports and challenges to their efforts to be involved in their children's parenting…' (Ly & Goldburg, 2014).

The results of this study show that fathers reported high depressive, anxious, and stress-related symptoms. Fathers were found to have low levels of participation in health-promoting activities. Fathers felt inhibited in their careers because of the care required by their child with disabilities. Fathers reported that, despite caring for their children, they received little support from services (which were mainly focused on mothers).

And yet. I was looking for the father's perspective.

Is this a naive attempt to contradict those who raise their eyebrows? Is it a search for the one white blackbird that throws all international (research) trends off the table? Or is it an attempt to learn from the father's perspective about the caring of men?

Caring of men is not always valued by the 'professional world'—some professionals (still) seem to target women/mothers in particular when it comes to caring messages and partnerships. Caring of men is also not taken seriously by academics—why else is there still such a modest focus on the fathers' perspective in academic research? Fathers who are carers are also not always respected by those who portray fathers in films and other media.

So we have a job to do!

Ghent, Belgium Geert Van Hove

References

Audenaert, V. (2023). *Gezinsenquête 2021: De taakverdeling thuis. Gezinnen in Vlaanderen over wie welke gezinstaken op zich neemt en hoe tevreden ze zijn met de verdeling van de gezinstaken*. Vlaamse overheid, Departement Welzijn, Volksgezondheid en Gezin. http://www.gezinsenquête.be

Bianchi, S. M., Milkie, M. A., Sayer, L. C., & Robinson, J. P. (2000). Is anyone doing the housework? Trends in the gender division of household labor. *Social Forces, 79*(1), 191–228.

Bourke-Taylor, H. M., Cotter, C., Joyce, K. S., Reddihough, D. S., & Brown, T. (2021). Fathers of children with a disability: Health, work, and family life issues. *Disability and Rehabilitation, 44*(16), 4441–4451. https://doi.org/10.1080/09638288.2021.1910739

Craig, L., & Mullan, K. (2011). How mothers and fathers share childcare: A cross-national time-use comparison. *American Sociological Review, 76*(6), 834–861.

Glorieux, I., Minnen, J., van Tienoven, T. P., Deyaert, J., & Mészáros, E. (2015). De (on)evenwichtige verdeling van arbeids- en gezinstaken tussen mannen en vrouwen. Evolutie en een stand van zaken. In B. Vanderheyden & M. Callens (Eds.), *Arbeid en Gezin: een paar apart* (pp. 45–65). SVR-studie.

Hochschild, A. R., & Machung, A. (1989). *The second shift: Working parents and the revolution at home*. Penguin Books.

Ly, A. R., & Goldberg, W. A. (2014). New measure for fathers of children with developmental challenges. *Journal of Intellectual Disability Research: JIDR, 58*(5), 471–484. https://doi.org/10.1111/jir.12044

Contents

1

Disability Studies (in Education) and Family Research

Abstract We learn in this chapter about the traditional research on families with children with disabilities and the influence of the medical model and its deficit mindset: families get pathologized. Stress and (mental) health and marital problems are attributed to families without giving attention to possible effects of experts, institutions, and power imbalances. Thinking from this mindset stereotypes about 'disabled families' living with a lower quality of life are reinforced. The only solution is 'to fix' these 'disabled families'.

Colleagues (also parents of children with disabilities) like Philip and Diane Ferguson, Linda Ware and Susan Gabel united in Disability Studies in Education highlighted the importance of understanding family dynamics from an insider perspective. They advocated for the promotion of social justice and the integration of family/parents' perspectives into the educational discourses. This integration could help us to recognize and respect diverse family experiences (emphasizing intersectional and contextual factors) making sure we get away from stigmatization. With this recognition, an inclusive and equitable approach to families through disability studies is introduced.

G. Van Hove, *Fathering Children with Disabilities*,
https://doi.org/10.1007/978-3-031-82960-4_1

Keywords Disability Studies (in Education) • Family Research • Medical model • Deficit mindset • Social justice • Intersectionality • Family Portraits • Stories • Mother-researchers

1.1 'Old School' Research

Researchers have always shown great interest in families with children with disabilities/labels. For years (and till now), this field of family research was conceived from a 'deficit mindset' (the well-known medical model[1]). Families with a child with a disability were positioned as 'disabled families'. The causes of problems and stress (Knussen & Sloper, 1992; Hsiao, 2018; Dervishaliaj, 2013) within these families were situated on the families themselves. In this research tradition, little or no attention was paid to the question of whether the experts (and by extension their institutions) were close enough to the families to (help them) deal with part of the problems; even more: whether the stress and problems were not (in)directly caused by the expert-professionals themselves.

Individualization (here at the family level) has historically provided the justification for the battery of institutions and services set up to address and solve 'the family problems' (Haydon-Laurelut, 2015). For a long time, families inscribed themselves into these research practices set up for 'the benefit of the common good'. Systematically, a corpus of data was thus built up with which the image of the 'disabled family' was repeatedly confirmed and deepened. Topics such as: stress, mental health problems, (a lower) Quality of Life, and divorce constituted the 'core' of these studies. Those family researchers and their teams succeeded in diverting attention from, for example, unequal power relations between experts and families OR the phenomenon of 'Othering' of children with disabilities and their families OR the inaccessibility of public space and

[1] The medicalization of disability refers to the power of medical professionals and the medical establishment that have been categorizing and labeling persons with disabilities as 'sick'. This model believes in the 'treatability' of persons with impairments (DasGupta, 2015, 120). This way of thinking and working can be directly linked to 'ableism' or the ideology that hyper valuates able-bodiedness and 'normalcy' (Campbell, 2015, 13).

public institutions (Lalvani & Polvere, 2013). Disability was 'treated', often in specialized institutions away from society and away from family life, natural networks, and the community. Disability became a phenomenon that families felt ashamed of, sought blame within the family, and many children (especially in rural areas) were 'kept at home' and not sent to school. They lived a kind of hidden life within the walls of the parental home.

1.2 Disability Studies?

And if, as stated in the preface, the emphasis in this book is not on the sociological or psychopathological angle, then what is the angle from which this book should be understood?

The title of this book makes it clear that we are radically committed to Disability Studies perspectives. We will briefly explain the basics of disability studies, as we do not assume that everyone is at home with this school of research.

Disability Studies (Van Hove, 2023) is an interdisciplinary field of study that critically examines the concept of disability, moving beyond the traditional medical/individual model to explore relational/social, cultural, political, and historical perspectives. In contrast to the medical/individual model, which focuses on the diagnosis, treatment or 'cure' of individuals, Disability Studies approaches disability as a complex construct. It is seen not as something 'of the individual' but as the result of a complex interaction between a person with an impairment or diagnosis and the physical, attitudinal, and systemic characteristics of the environments and cultures in which people live.

Central to Disability Studies is the idea that society should be inclusive and accessible to all. The field examines how laws, policies, environments, media representations, and cultural attitudes (full of ableist perspectives) shape the living conditions and experiences of people with disabilities and their families. Disability Studies also emphasizes the importance of the voices and perspectives (lived experiences) of persons with disabilities and advocates for the self-representation and empowerment of persons with disabilities.

Disability Studies increasingly intersects with other fields such as Gender Studies, Queer Theory, Critical Race Studies, Post-/Decolonial Studies, and Migration Studies to explore how disability interacts with other identities such as race, gender, and class.

An important focus within Disability Studies is the human rights approach. We see the United Nations Convention on the Rights of Persons with Disabilities (2006, UNCRPD) as a foundational document of rights that underpins a global movement to protect, provide, and ensure the participation of citizens.

At Ghent University, within Disability Studies, we put a lot of emphasis on the relational perspective, in parallel with the human rights perspective. Together with Dokumacı (2019) and other researchers, we believe that besides 'big activism' and 'big actions', much attention should also be paid to small performances that show that disabled people and their immediate environment are not passive, but creative. This parallel attention allows for improvising and allying with people who 'see' and 'feel' the needs of others. (Mia Mingus calls this 'access intimacy', see also later in this book.)

In addition to its academic importance, Disability Studies is also transformative in nature, advocating for changes in the way in which society conceptualizes and interacts with disability. It challenges stigmatizing narratives and promotes a more inclusive understanding. Disability is seen as a natural part of human diversity. Changes in areas like architecture, public policy, healthcare, and education encourage society to value the contributions and rights of people with disabilities.

1.3 The Times They Are A-changing

Fortunately, there has been a reversal in the picture outlined so far. An extremely important group of Disability Studies scholars has played a major role in this turnaround. These are academics who are also fathers/mothers of children with disabilities. Some of these colleagues who have done pioneering work found each other in the Disability Studies in Education network (Allan, 2020). We introduce the work of some of them below.

Philip and Diane Ferguson regularly delivered texts that are visionary in terms of the 'different position' that parents and families of people with disabilities can take.

In an important article from 2001, Philip Ferguson presents the major research orientations that developed over the last century concerning family reactions to having a child with a disability (p. 124). He describes that in the nineteenth to the early twentieth century, families with children with disabilities were mainly dismissed as families who were 'disrupting the moral code'. With a mix of emerging knowledge of genetics and morality, the main argument was to prevent 'those families' from bringing any more children into the world as well as to take the children away from families: professionals with all their expertise would take over the tasks of these 'unworthy' parents.

In most of the twentieth century, the focus on families changed: the main focus came to be on how these children with disabilities affect the course of events in their families; even how they damage their families. The focus shifted from the child with disabilities to also looking at their families who needed 'therapeutic interventions' … for their shame, their guilt, their denial, their conflicts about taking on different roles, the impact on the quality of the marital relationship of parents, social isolation, and so on (p. 125).

Influenced by different psychological schools, different images of parents thus emerge: the neurotic parent, the dysfunctional parent, the suffering parent, the powerless parent (pp. 126–127).

From the 1980s onwards, a new trend emerged: families received more and more support, for instance from early intervention services (p. 127). This evolution helps in doing more and more research (p. 128) into those processes that show how some families creatively adapt to the extra-questions and extra-care that a child with a disability entails. This different way of looking at families bears many opportunities to get away from the tunnel vision that lumps all 'those' families together. Specific experiences linked to socio-economic situation, to culture, to religion, are taken seriously and show that an intersectional approach is emerging.

In the 2013 text 'Family Portraits', Phil and Diane Ferguson make a razor-sharp analysis of the representation of families in basic training manuals for students who will later work in 'special education'. First and foremost—and this is the good news—the Fergusons discovered that more and more attention is being paid to families in those textbooks. A purely quantitative content analysis of the books shows that texts on families or parents are regularly covered in a 'separate chapter' and that texts on families usually do not make up more than 3–5% of the text material of such a book (p. 153). Treating family life separately in separate chapters: the Fergusons see it as a contradiction to the much-discussed important input of parents-as-real-partners or input as experts by experience in moments of dialogue regarding pedagogical processes to support their children.

The Fergusons make a case for connecting 'special education' to discussions that have been taking place in mainstream schools for some time (p. 153). In particular, there has been a shift from 'parent participation-for-the-pedagogical-added-value' to a discourse that seeks social justice for parents and the communities in which they live and work, in addition to the extra value to students in schools.

Linda Ware—one of the founding mothers of Disability Studies in Education—describes in an essay back in 2006 (pp. 1–2) what differences can be made by having in place systems of administration and budget systems for persons with disabilities. For example, she sees her son flourishing (thanks to) in the special culture of the state of New Mexico. Care staff there appear to work with great passion; construction promoters appear to be less pressured by bureaucratic interferences.

On a personal-relational level (p. 2), she 'draws' her relationship with her son as alternating between struggle and solidarity. In Ware's texts, it becomes clear that despite all the peculiarities, mothers mainly take on roles that are universally recognizable, for example, 'The advocate', but also 'the intruder' (p. 3).

In a preface to the book 'Constructing the (M)Other' (Lalvani, 2019), Ware describes that mothers everywhere are surrounded, as it were, by discourses on 'a good mother' and 'the desirable child' (xiii). Many mothers try day by day to question or challenge those 'normalizing ideologies'.

Ware is a strong advocate of working through stories. Stories that introduce us to the complex, real life and that do not degenerate into 'vignettes' or even worse 'case studies'. Such stories are told and retold; in this way, mothers are helped to give meaning/seek meaning in/to the things they do with their children and the decisions they make with their 'special child'.

One of the most influential authors within Disability Studies in Education is undoubtedly **Susan Gabel.**[2] Among other things, she has managed to unite a group of 'mother-researchers' and build with them an insight into families with children with disabilities specifically from a mother's perspective.

In a 2010 text she co-wrote with Jan Valle (also a mother-researcher), she asks profound questions about the (cultural, social, and political) context in which mothers have to raise their children (p. 187).

In doing so, Valle and Gabel particularly studied what happens when the phenomenon of 'disability' threatens to disrupt the cultural script for motherhood (p. 188). This script is developing in an American middle-class culture that the authors describe as: '…the ultimate competition for rapidly shrinking resources…' (p. 189). This competitive atmosphere creates a lot of anxiety, turmoil (will I (still) be able to give my children the best?). and stress. (Some middle-class parents are looking for 'the best' daycare center even before their children are born to ensure the best starting position). This kind of strategic planning behavior—on top of the average mother/parent tasks—leads to a kind of social cascade: the more (p. 190) we fear for our children, the more anxious we become. And the more anxious we are, the more protective we become. The more protective

[2] Susan Gabel is at the moment Professor in Inclusive Education at Wayne State University in Detroit.

we are, the more we believe in our capacity to keep our children safe from the ills of the world. So this is how helicopter parents are born.

According to Valle and Gabel, the institutions, such as schools, of society are fully involved in this merry-go-round. Children are expected to perform at a very early age and thus ‘meet the standards’. A ‘mythical normal child’ is created against which all children are measured. In their attempts to come up with solutions and fix children, schools and their professionals are constantly observing, documenting, analyzing, and categorizing (p. 198). Mothers of children with disabilities are therefore confronted with test results, with labels and diagnoses, with interventions and with referrals (p. 194). Many mothers also hesitate to share questions they have about their children with the institutions just because this might trigger certain testing machinations. These machineries often lead to loss of control for parents (who have to leave the upbringing of their children to experts) (p. 196). Some mothers feel blamed (certain experts suggest they have not yet accepted their child’s disability) (p. 197) the moment they do not blindly follow the paths laid out for them.

All this leads to the intrusion of the question into their ordinary lives of whether they can be a ‘good enough’ mother (p. 198).

In a 2018 text, Gabel, together with Kathy Kotel, builds on. Here, the impact of previously described processes is analyzed from the birth of children with visible disabilities (in this article: Down Syndrome).

Already from childbirth, we hear mothers describe practices that we will kindly describe as ‘inappropriate fumbling’. Some care workers represent ‘the hostile world’ in which mothers and their children will find themselves. Images of mothers who do not live up to the ‘ideal image of the good mother’ are conjured up by those practices. This can be compounded by the denial of the personhood of the new babies by those same care workers.

These stories are a far cry from the rose-tinted stories surrounding births.

An illustration to conclude this chapter. We couldn’t have described it better ourselves.

Parent perspectives on inclusive education for students with intellectual disability: A scoping review of the literature
Jordan Shurr, Alexandra Minuk, Mona Holmqvist, Daniel Östlund, Nehal Ghaith and Brenda Reed

Abstract

The aim of this study was to collect and analyze research on inclusive education from the perspective of parents of students with intellectual disability (ID). The review examined characteristics and trends related to geographical origin of research, design, data collection, publication source and year, source of data, age of individuals with ID, and research focus. The initial database search produced a total of 2540 non-duplicated articles published between 1994 and 2019. In total, 63 articles were included from the initial search and a subsequent ancestry search. The results show a significant increase in publication on the topic in the final one-tenth of the review time parameter, suggesting a continued upward trend. The majority of articles were qualitative in design, used interviews and surveys to collect data, and focus on the perspectives and beliefs of parents on inclusive education. Gaps in the existing set of research included a lack of family perspectives beyond that of mothers (e.g. father, grandparent) and a limited focus beyond perspectives and beliefs, to that of parent experiences of inclusive education.
Source: International Journal on Developmental Disabilities, 2023, 69 (5), 633–643. https://doi.org/10.1080/20473869.2021.2003612

References

Allan, J. (2020). Disability studies and interdisciplinarity: Interregnum of productive interruption? In L. Ware (Ed.), *Critical readings in interdisciplinary disability studies* (pp. 5–17). Springer.

Campbell, F. K. (2015). Ability. In R. Adams, B. Reiss, & D. Serlin (Eds.), *Keywords for disability studies* (pp. 12–14). New York University Press.

DasGupta, S. (2015). Medicalization. In R. Adams, B. Reiss, & D. Serlin (Eds.), *Keywords for disability studies* (pp. 120–121). New York University Press.

Dervishaliaj, E. (2013). Parental stress in families of children with disabilities: A literature review. *Journal of Educational and Social Research, 3*(7), 579. https://doi.org/10.5901/jesr.2013.v3n7p579

Dokumacı, A. (2019). A theory of microactivist affordances. *South Atlantic Quarterly, 118*, 491–519. https://doi.org/10.1215/00382876-7616127

Ferguson, D. L., Ferguson, P. M., Kim, J., & Li, C. (2013). Family portraits: Past and present representations of parents in special education textbooks. In L. Ware & R. Slee (Eds.), *Ellen A. Brantlinger: When meaning falters and words fail, ideology matters* (pp. 144–165). Brill/Sense.

Ferguson, P. M. (2001). Mapping the family: Narrative patterns in family portrayals of disability. In G. Albrecht, K. D. Seelman, & M. Bury (Eds.), *Handbook of disability studies* (pp. 373–395). Sage Publications.

Gabel, S. L., & Kotel, K. (2018). Motherhood in the context of normative discourse: Birth stories of mothers of children with Down syndrome. *Journal of Medical Humanities, 39*(2), 179–193.

Haydon-Laurelut, M. (2015). Disability beyond individualization, psychologisation and medicalization. *Metalogos, 27*, 1–15.

Hsiao, Y.-J. (2018). Parental stress in families of children with disabilities. *Intervention in School and Clinic, 53*(4), 201–205. https://doi.org/10.1177/1053451217712956

Knussen, C., & Sloper, P. (1992). Stress in families of children with disability: A review of risk and resistance factors. *Journal of Mental Health, 1*(3), 241–256. https://doi.org/10.3109/09638239209005457

Lalvani, P. (Ed.). (2019). *Constructing the (M)other: Narratives of disability, motherhood and the politics of normal.* Peter Lang Publishing.

Lalvani, P., & Polvere, L. (2013). Historical perspectives on studying families of children with disabilities: A case for critical research. *Disability Studies Quarterly, 33*(3).

Valle, J. W., & Gabel, S. (2010). The sirens of normative mythology: Mother narratives of engagement and resistance. In C. Dudley-Marling (Ed.), *Deconstructing the normal curve and reconstructing the education for students with disabilities* (pp. 187–204). Peter Lang.

Van Hove, G. (2023). Disability Studies: Even a young field of science has a history. *Sartonia, 36*, 117–164.

Ware, L. (2006). Diego's life without her. *Equity and Excellence in Education, 39*, 1–3.

Ware, L. (2019). There was this mother, one mother.... In P. Lalvani (Ed.), *Constructing the (M)other: Narratives of disability, motherhood and the politics of normal* (pp. xiii–xv). Peter Lang.

2

Some First Paternal Perspectives Appearing in the Scientific Literature

Abstract This chapter provides an overview of the growing number of articles that explore the lives of fathers of children with disabilities. We attempt to synthesize findings from 11 different review articles—published between 2013 and 2023—based on literature reviews, systematic reviews, meta-analyses, or meta-syntheses.

So far, the focus seems to be on deficits and labels. A more sensitive father-inclusive research project is needed to give a more nuanced picture of the experiences of the father and to better understand and support the multiple roles of fathers in families with children with disabilities.

Keywords Scientific Literature • Fathers • Deficits and labels • Perspectives • Support • Review studies

Despite the long absence or scarcity of fathers' perspectives in research on children with disabilities, there is an increasing number of publications that focus specifically on fathers, their role, and their position in families with children with disabilities.

G. Van Hove, *Fathering Children with Disabilities*,
https://doi.org/10.1007/978-3-031-82960-4_2

In this chapter, we try to give an initial picture of the image of fathers in the research literature. We followed a very specific strategy.

First, we used articles that were either literature reviews, systematic reviews, meta-analyses, or meta-syntheses. Literature reviews generally don't have the same methodological rigor as systematic reviews. Unlike systematic reviews, they don't aim to answer a clinical question. Literature reviews can help to contextualize or background new research.

Some articles also used meta-analysis or meta-synthesis. Meta-analysis and synthesis are two common methods of data analysis in research management. Both aim to integrate and summarize findings from studies on a topic or question. Synthesis is a qualitative or mixed-methods technique that synthesizes findings across studies using thematic or narrative methods. Meta-analysis is a quantitative technique that combines the results of several independent studies by means of statistical methods.

We used 11 reviews published in the last 10 years (oldest 2013, most recent 2023). Taken together, these studies make up a total of 596 articles. This size allows us to say that, without ignoring some duplication, we are very likely to be able to base this chapter on the available research literature on fathers and children with disabilities.

The systematic review by Lopez et al. (2019) focuses in particular on fathers' involvement with pre-school aged children.

It is striking that comparisons between studies become very problematic due to the different ways in which fathers' 'involvement' is measured/identified in the studies reviewed by these authors (57–59).

When comparing the involvement of fathers between groups of children with and without a disability, fathers are less involved than mothers in both cases, that is, the presence of a diagnosis does not make a difference in terms of involvement.

It was also noted that there is still a lot to be gained in terms of the involvement of fathers in what is referred to as 'family based interventions'. Mothers tend to be seen as the first to get involved in these interventions.

In terms of getting fathers more involved, these authors put a lot of faith in early intervention and home support services. These services could already play an important role at the level of information, for example, by informing fathers about the unique opportunities they can have in the upbringing and development of their child.

Childcare centers and (kindergarten) schools could do more to involve fathers by scheduling parental meetings so that fathers working outdoors can attend more easily.

They also point to interesting research showing that family activities with special attention/actions for fathers are more effective than organizing 'men/fathers only' activities.

From the research, they also draw attention to divorced parents, whose income sometimes prevents them from staying at home longer and caring for their children during this time.

The research shows: Some fathers are at risk of getting lost in the world of specialist services and therapeutic settings. There also seems to be a great deal of potential for improvement in making these settings more accessible to fathers as well.

It is worth noting that three of the reviews have an explicit focus on fathers of children with an autism spectrum disorder.

Already in 2013, Braunstein and colleagues (1) showed that fathers were significantly underrepresented in research with families of children with Autism Spectrum Disorder (858). This was also the case in the research on older children with autism. It was still initially thought that mothers, as an important figure with young children, would come into balance with fathers when the children were older; this was not the case (861). When older studies were compared with more recent ones (862), the same stable trend—low father presence—was observed.

In reviewing the literature, Braunstein et al. tried to explain what caused this.

One possible explanation was related to the higher rate of divorce in families with a child with autism. Another possible explanation is 'habit formation' among researchers (863–864): for years people have been used to addressing mothers more conveniently in data collection. This often manifests itself in research practice; many studies provide only one interview/questionnaire form per family (which does not encourage the collection of two different perspectives) (864).

All this, according to Braunstein et al., leads to the danger that in practice people must work with fathers without a thorough knowledge of their needs and requirements (and then simply erroneously continue to 'translate' their approach from mothers to fathers) (864).

The tension between a broader (even almost disability studies-based) style of analysis (Lascewicz et.al.) on the one hand and a more deficit-oriented style (Rankin et.al.) on the other is illustrated by two articles from 2019.

Lashewicz et al. (2019) find that fathers' lives are affected by their children with autism; some of them report, for example, that the fact that their child does not (yet) have a diagnosis has put a strain on their relationship with their partner. Some fathers also complain that there are few accommodations and compensations available that would make it easier for them to reconcile their work situation with the parental responsibilities that they would like to take on (126). From our disability studies perspective, we are also very pleased that this review brings in elements that go beyond deficit thinking: fathers point to the possibilities that the child offers for enjoying 'little things'; some fathers also see their child as a key to understanding difference (128). These authors are in favor of specific forums where fathers can post and share their adaptations and solutions.

In this review, special attention is also given to fathers from 'other' cultures. It argues for a culturally sensitive approach to fathers (recognizing that cultural backgrounds, along with language differences, can add important layers to the isolation some fathers feel) (128). At the same time, it urges against falling into the trap of cultural stereotyping under the guise of cultural sensitivity (129).

The focus of the article by Rankin et al. (2019) is on fathers and, specifically, their contribution to the development of their children with autism. In view of the field of research covered by this journal (clinical psychology, child psychopathology), the emphasis is on a kind of co-therapist role for parents. A deficit-oriented atmosphere pervades this entire review (role of fathers in supporting and developing communication, in supporting what are described as comorbid psychiatric disorders) (458).

Consistent with the above, the absence of fathers from 'parent training interventions' is very noticeable to these authors (459).

The stress of couples with children with autism is highlighted, as are the sometimes 'father-unfriendly' hours of counselling and support (the sessions are organized during the day, which often does not fit in with the working hours of the fathers) (459).

Clearly, in addition to the deficit orientation, the authors also assume more traditional maternal and paternal roles in parenting.

Despite this, the authors claim (460) that change is urgently needed, given that fathers are increasingly indicating that they want to be involved in raising their children (with autism).

Looking at studies where fathers have been involved in treatment/ guidance, the authors can only be optimistic: fathers seem to be able to implement the proposed (often behavioral) interventions with their children properly (474).

Three reviews address the situation of fathers of children with intellectual disabilities.

Using 27 research studies, Davys et al. (2017) have produced a review based on the perspective that paternal involvement in raising and supporting their disabled children can have a positive effect on their involvement throughout the life course. The authors' view is that children with intellectual disabilities need lifelong support and that fathers have a role to play.

The review shows that many fathers experienced the diagnosis of their child as a severe shock, they first had to go through a period of confusion (during which they had to adjust the image of the 'child of their dreams'). Fortunately, many fathers indicate that they adapted to their child with intellectual disability during the first years after the diagnosis. In this way, they were still able to fulfil their role as fathers.

A lot of fathers seem to be very worried about the future of their child: will there be enough good support available for them? Will there be a good place for their child to live in later? Will there be a sufficiently stable financial situation for the family and the child? And when their son or daughter leaves school, what will happen to them?

Differences, even contradictions, were found in the various articles on which the review was based (both in comparative research with other groups of fathers and within the group of fathers of children with disabilities): for example, differences can be observed in the level of stress in fathers' lives. Differences can also be observed in terms of marital satisfaction or divorce.

The various studies within the reviewed literature do not provide a clear answer to the question of whether there is a relationship between fathers' involvement on the one hand and possible effects on children's development on the other.

The authors of this review note that in many places fathers still have very little involvement in communication about their children with intellectual disabilities. They are therefore in favor of special 'father moments' where fathers can share experiences with other fathers. They also call for more research involving fathers of adult children—as many studies do not include this group.

Based on the observation that fathers are increasingly expected to be actively involved in caring for and educating their intellectually disabled children, Dunn et al. (2019) sought to investigate whether this involvement affects their mental health. To do this, they compared the situation of fathers with mothers of an intellectually disabled child and fathers in general.

Despite all the efforts of fathers to become more involved (in reality they often still play a more modest role), it seems that it is mainly mothers who suffer from mental health problems. Fathers often remain the 'breadwinner', with mothers staying at home or taking up part-time work. Among mothers, the main protective factors against mental health problems appear to relate to work outside the home. In addition, the latter—mothers working outside the home—does not always seem to have an impact on fathers taking on more caring responsibilities.

Living without too many financial worries and experiencing social support turned out to be mediators of fathers' mental health and well-being.

The occurrence of challenging behavior in children also seems to lead to more mental health problems in the parents (and therefore in the fathers).

It is also good to have a systematic review—Thakkar, 2023—that looks specifically at fathers of children with Down Syndrome. Dunn et al. (2019, 7) refer to the 'Down Syndrome advantage' when looking at the mental health of the parents of these children—they seem to do better than parents of children with intellectual disabilities without Down Syndrome. Explanations vary: the parents of these children are on average older and often have fewer financial problems; other studies suggest that these children on average show less challenging behavior.

In addition to the shock of the diagnosis, he fear of the future and the impact of the continuing stigma of disability that has been reported in previous studies, this author also allows space for the fathers to talk about the 'rewards' (23–25): the fathers had stories about building a bond with their children and how this motivated them to continue to be involved in their children's development. Furthermore, when looking at the (sometimes small) steps their children were taking, the fathers showed a lot of pride. In addition to the many barriers of stigma, receiving much support from other families or professionals was perceived as a great reward for many parents. Dads also spoke about their personal growth and changing attitudes toward disability because of dealing with their children; this was also perceived as a reward.

We have three overviews that look at fathering in specific child groups: Sujalmo and Chusairi (2023) zoom in on father–child relationships with a specific interest into fathers living in 'rural areas'; Spurr et al. (2023) explore how fathers of children with 'chronic illness conditions' experience caring for their children; and Szarkowski and Dirks (2021) focus on fathers of deaf and hard of hearing children. It is also fascinating to have a closer look at these—often less high-profile—'groups' in comparison to children with autism or children with intellectual disabilities. So, we discuss them below, study by study.

Sujalmo and Chusairi (2023), two Indonesian authors who wanted to identify factors influencing rural fathers' involvement, admit that they found very little literature on the subject. As a result, many of their suggestions are not robust and stable enough to be considered real conclusions.

However, there are two lines from their overview which, in our opinion, could be decisive with regard to the position of fathers 'in rural areas'.

The authors point out that the inclusion of the father's role in the literature they studied is often linked to contextual factors: they mention (6433) cultural customs, family relationships, socio-economic status, the job in which the father works, and the social networks in which the father is involved or not involved. The authors also draw attention to the stigmatization of children with disabilities and the particular impact of this phenomenon on father involvement.

Spurr et al. (2023) looked at the experiences of fathers of children with chronic illness. (Among the studies they reviewed serious liver disease, asthma, diabetes, cystic fibrosis, phenylketonuria, cancer, nephrological diseases, juvenile rheumatoid arthritis, inflammatory bowel disease, which are mentioned as examples of chronic illness.)

It is striking that in families with a child with a chronic illness, the role of primary caregiver still seems to fall to the mother.

The authors also call for more specific research into the possible impact on the mental health of fathers of children with chronic illnesses, and in particular on fathers who take on (co)caring roles.

The authors emphasize that the moment when fathers become (more) involved in the care of a child with a chronic illness, there are immediate needs for (additional) support from within and outside the family. The authors propose concrete actions, as well as additional initiatives to inform and train fathers in the care of a child with a chronic illness.

Szarkowski and Dirks (2021) help us to understand the situation of fathers of deaf and hard of hearing children.

Although the first publications on the subject date from 50 years ago (195), these authors paint a picture of a collection of data on fathers that has 'only scratched the surface'. They therefore advocate continuing to look for the 'unique' experiences and contributions made by fathers.

Here too, and this is strongly influenced by the cultural context in which the studies were carried out, mothers in particular were seen as the coordinators of the children's care (arranging and keeping appointments for support and medical care, being involved in support schemes).

In studies with very young deaf and hard of hearing children (195), it was found that fathers' involvement in daily routines and early supervision of their children led to greater paternal self-efficacy (also leading to a more qualitative relationship with their partner).

Among this group of children, interesting research differences were also observed among fathers who were themselves deaf: for example, they included more waiting time in their attempts to increase the child's involvement in communication. These deaf fathers would also achieve higher quality back and forth communication moments with their young children (p. 193)—as was observed during initiating visual communication strategies with 2-year-olds.

Finally, let us mention the very comprehensive and interesting meta-analysis of Shorey and Pereira (2023), authors who have focused on the experiences of fathers of children with 'neurodevelopmental disorders' (IDD, ASD, ADHD, specific learning difficulties, etc.). This is because the study looks in detail at the future perspectives of fathers.

Many fathers report having had a difficult start with their children (p. 758)—is my child different? Do we need to look for a diagnosis for this child? The image of losing the 'perfect child' brings confusion and difficult questions.

A lot of fathers also report that it is not easy to navigate a complex landscape of specialist services and professionals (pp. 760–761).

Fathers in the 38 collected studies struggle with the 'idealized father role' (762–765) and all that is expected in a masculine image of strong men. Many of them come a long way by forming coalitions with their partners, with their family and friends, with professionals. These steps help (765–767) to adjust the expectations they have of their child. This often runs parallel to adjusting their own position and the roles they take on. Fathers feel that they have grown and dare to think about a future for their children (767). It is striking that the dreams they hold for their children seem to parallel the dreams they hold for a 'better world':

- A school and health care system that is more accessible to all
- A world with more compassion for those that are different
- A world where their children can participate and build a life away from their parents

At the end of these reviews, several themes emerge that raise questions about whether we have really learned more about fathers' experiences in relation to their children. For example, the focus on diagnoses is striking; one wonders whether this deficit thinking is not often a distraction from what is really important. In addition, there are many examples of authors in danger of getting completely lost in positioning fathers in a 'suffering role'. The hard life image then wins out over enjoying each other and the little things in life.

References

Braunstein, V. L., Peniston, N., Perelman, A., & Cassano, M. C. (2013). The inclusion of fathers in investigations of autistic spectrum disorders. *Research in Autism Spectrum Disorders, 7,* 858–868.

Davys, D., Mitchell, D., & Martin, R. (2017). Fathers of people with intellectual disability: A review of the literature. *Journal of Intellectual Disabilities, 21*(2), 175–196. https://doi.org/10.1177/1744629516650129

Dunn, K., Kinnear, D., Jahoda, A., & McConnachie, A. (2019). Mental health and well-being of fathers of children with intellectual disabilities: Systematic review and meta-analysis. *BJPsych Open, 5*(6), e96. https://doi.org/10.1192/bjo.2019.75

Lashewicz, B. M., Shipton, L., & Lien, K. (2019). Meta-synthesis of fathers' experiences raising children on the autism spectrum. *Journal of Intellectual Disabilities, 23*(1), 117–131.

Lopez, S., McWhirter, A. C., Rosencrans, M., Giuliani, N. R., & McIntyre, L. L. (2019). Father involvement with children with developmental delays. *Global Education Review, 6*(1), 40–62.

Rankin, J. A., Paisley, C. A., Tomeny, T. S., & Eldred, S. W. (2019). Fathers of youth with autism spectrum disorder: A systematic review of the impact of fathers' involvement on youth, families, and intervention. *Clinical Child and Family Psychology Review, 22*(4), 458–477. https://doi.org/10.1007/s10567-019-00294-0

Shorey, S., & Pereira, T. L.-B. (2023). Experiences of fathers caring for children with neurodevelopmental disorders: A meta-synthesis. *Family Process, 62,* 754–774. https://doi.org/10.1111/famp.12817

Spurr, S., Danford, C. A., Roberts, K. J., Sheppard-LeMoine, D., Machado Silva-Rodrigues, F., Darezzo Rodrigues Nunes, M., Darmofal, L., Ersig, A. L., Foster, M., Giambra, B., et al. (2023). Fathers' experiences of caring for a child with a chronic illness: A systematic review. *Children, 10*(2), 197. https://doi.org/10.3390/children10020197

Sujalmo, A., & Chusairi, A. (2023). Determinant factors of father involvement in early childhood with disabilities: A systematic review. *Jurnal Obsesi: Jurnal Pendidikan Anak Usia Dini, 7*(5), 6428–6438. https://doi.org/10.31004/obsesi.v7i5.5472

Szarkowski, A., & Dirks, E. (2021). Fathers of young deaf or hard-of-hearing children: A systematic review. *Journal of Deaf Studies and Deaf Education, 26*(2), 187–208. https://doi.org/10.1093/deafed/enaa039

Thakkar, D. (2023). *Systematic review of fathers' attitudes toward their children with Down syndrome: A lifespan approach from infancy to midlife* (Master's thesis, Jönköping University).

3

Famous Fathers of Children with Disabilities

Abstract This chapter presents two historical case studies of General Charles de Gaulle and philosopher John Dewey, both fathers of children with disabilities. Their personal experiences, societal challenges, and the impact of their children on their professional and personal lives are described.

Both famous personalities have demonstrated personal growth through their close relationships with their children. We don't see much impact when we examine the transfer of insights from personal to public life. Both cases show that disability as a phenomenon in these case studies remains private (family) and does not necessarily have much political or theoretical impact.

Keywords Famous fathers • Historical case studies • Down Syndrome • Inclusion • Stigma • Fatherhood • Legacy • Eugenics

I am a firm believer in the fact that there is a great deal to be learned from our history. So, what can we learn from a world leader AND an internationally renowned philosopher-psychologist-pedagogue? Two interesting historical figures are positioned specifically because they were fathers of children with disabilities.

G. Van Hove, *Fathering Children with Disabilities*,
https://doi.org/10.1007/978-3-031-82960-4_3

3.1 General de Gaulle

Disclaimer

This chapter is based on reference books about de Gaulle and his family (Neau-Dufour, 2010; Clerc, 2000), but also on photos and interviews (those can be found in the de Gaulle museum).

The question we must ask ourselves is whether the image of the general is a true one OR whether we are being led into a chapter of total praise, as is often the case with hero worship. Either we read this story as an example of a father who, at the beginning of the twentieth century, took responsibility and did everything he could to make the life of his daughter within the family as good as possible. Or we can read this story as an exaggeration that has to fit into the overall picture of the French hero.

The choice is up to the reader.

General Charles de Gaulle is regarded by many French citizens as the greatest Frenchman of all time. However, the military man, who gave much of his life for La France with extreme discipline and is also perceived as such by everyone, also had a soft side. The back cover of the book 'Les de Gaulle, une famille Française' highlights this very explicitly. Little Anne, the child 'like no other', revealed the hidden tenderness of the General.[1]

Anne, whom nobody at the time knew during pregnancy would be diagnosed with Down Syndrome, was expected with great joy as we can read (Clerc, 2000, 125). At the end of the summer of the year 1927, Jeanne de Gaulle (mother of Charles) decided to go on a pilgrimage with her three sons, Xavier, Charles, and Pierre, because they survived the war. Jeanne wants to pay homage to Mother Mary with the family at Lourdes. Yvonne, Charles' wife, does not travel with them because she is pregnant for the third time; 'L'heureux événement' is expected for late December-early January.

[1] About the 'other side' of Charles de Gaulle his personality we read following observation: …When the nephews and nieces visited their uncle and aunt, they would notice that Uncle Jacques would get tender and take Anne on his lap, noticing that she would pinch and slap his cheeks, leaving red marks. But he, with an incredible patience that he would never have with his eldest son Philippe, not even with his little daughter Elisabeth (aged six and four when Anne was born), sang her endless children's or military songs (Clerc, 126).

Anne was born on 1 January 1928. Immediately after birth, it was noticed that the little baby had unusual features on her eyes and mouth. People were also concerned about her physical stiffness. The de Gaulle family was close to Professor Lévy-Solal,[2] one of the country's top gynecologists, who saw very quickly and confirmed that Anne had Down Syndrome.

It is striking how defeatist and negative the reaction to the diagnosis of Down Syndrome was at the time (all this takes place in early 1928). Let us read along with the family story: the baby has Down Syndrome and all treatments are useless. Not only will she not grow normally, but she will always be severely handicapped: unable to say three words; unable to feed herself, as she will keep her milk teeth and will only be able to eat puréed food; unable to see an obstacle, as her eyesight is very poor and she cannot wear glasses; unable to see the danger posed by fire, water, glass, or

[2] In 1917, he was appointed to lead a sector in the North. At Calais Hospital, he met the woman who was to become his wife. It was also there that he made friends with the Vendroux family, one of whose daughters, Yvonne, became the wife of Charles de Gaulle, a friend of Lévy-Solal (https://cths.fr/an/savant.php?id=4124#).

any other obstacle. Gentle, desperate for affection, especially from her father. But prone to nervous outbursts and, once calmed, sudden gestures (125).

It is striking how many times 'unable' is emphasized in this description.

At age 38, General de Gaulle was clearly going through a major crisis. He was a deeply religious man. Until then, he had full confidence in his future and his mission for his country. But this confidence was literally swept away by the birth of his youngest daughter.

Let us add another excerpt from the family book. Why did this have to happen to him and his family? Who is responsible? Was it him who might have been carrying some kind of hidden defect in his body? Was it God who sent him this child as a kind of mission? Disability was not unknown to him, as one of his brothers (Jacques) was physically impaired.[3] If only it was that, but no, it was 'mental'. Just 'the mind', just what he himself considered the greatest good. Was it God who wanted to punish him? But why did he have to be punished? (127–128).

> … Up to that point, the general had not known how much a human being could suffer. Nor did he know until that moment, how much tenderness this baby was capable of awakening in him…. As soon as he heard Anne make a sound, he dropped everything—he might even have been writing a letter or a note for his marshal… He loved nothing more than to take her in his arms and hold her, to soothe her, to sing to her…. (128)

According to the chronicler of the family, Christine Clerc, the General, now almost 40 years old, had become a completely different person. Charles (p. 135) tried to follow the spirit of his father (the very patient and amiable Prof Henri de Gaulle), but he found it difficult, and occasionally he really went off the rails. For example, he always showed great impatience when it came to punctuality—anecdotes circulate that he often left alone for church on Sunday mornings because he could not bring himself to wait for his wife and children to finish—and we know that he could be very colicky toward his son Philippe if his schoolwork

---

[3] Charles' younger brother Jacques was stricken with lethargic encephalitis in 1926. Since then, his paralysis had been steadily progressing and would soon force the civil engineer of the Mines Department and father of three children to give up his job.

did not go smoothly (he is said to have occasionally thrown books at his son). He was often a little more kind to his daughter Elisabeth, because she turned out to be such a good student, but it is only Anne who seems to really arouse his tenderness. He became a man who, from now on, would always keep a part of his attention free for the education and the well-being of his daughter.

In family stories circulating about cousins visiting Colombey (p. 140), we read that the General liked to ask the children at table trick questions and riddles. He also liked to take them for walks in the fields around the estate. At the end of the afternoon, Charles disappears from the company and can be found upstairs in Anne's room. Anyone listening carefully hears father and daughter laughing and singing children's songs like 'Savez vous planter les choux?'

It is also notable that in letters to family members (137–138), Charles often writes explicitly about Anne (thus not erasing her from the family history). For example, in a letter to his favorite niece, he writes that Philippe and Elisabeth are back at school after the Christmas holidays and that they are both doing very well. And Anne is getting better too, he writes, she is trying to go through life more balanced and calmer. In his eyes, she is still the 'pauvre enfant anormale'. But he is beginning to discover her personality more and more.

The major changes in the General's personality were evident in several areas. These included several important decisions. Some of those decisions were very concrete.

Part of Anne's education was entrusted to a nurse (Miss Potel); not surprisingly, such a person was not easy to locate. It is when the family chronicle their departure for Lebanon that we first read of Miss Potel. In 1929, the de Gaulle family left for Lebanon. Yvonne's parents accompanied them to the station to begin the long journey. They were accompanied by their two children, Philippe and Elisabeth (aged 8 and 5 at the time), and by Anne, the 'little sick child', almost 2 years old and accompanied by Mademoiselle Potel, the governess-nurse. Not much is known about the governess and nurse Marguerite Potel. Neau-Dufour's book tells us that the governess looked after Anne until 1947, when she retired after 15 years of loyal service. Potel was at her disposal around the clock and became a real member of the family. To get an idea of this woman's closeness to Anne, it is interesting to magnify the following detail: in one of the family's many moving plans, we read the following—'Anne, aged four, needs a private room, especially as her governess sleeps next to her.' Later, Miss Potel moved with them several times and continued to accompany Anne. She lives with her at the family estate at la Colombey, but also follows the family during the war to 'safer places' in France (with Charles' sister), to England and to Algiers. The governess was apparently entitled to 1 month's leave (in August), as can be deduced from the fact that a replacement had to be found. On her retirement, her replacement was a local widow, Mrs Michignaud, but Anne died a few months after her retirement.

Anne was never placed in an institution; she always stayed with the family. For Anne to grow up in a healthy and peaceful environment, the family bought an estate in the Vosges Mountains. The village of Colombey-les-Deux-Eglises is still inextricably linked to Charles De Gaulle and his family. The family home can be visited, and a large museum has been built nearby in honor of the former president. Situated in a quiet corner of France, the De Gaulles found peace during their family moments. During the periods they spent there, the family sought and found harmony with the rhythms and customs of the simple village, where the church and the dignitaries determined everything. Above all, however, the small country estate was a safe place for Anne to grow up in.

It is also noteworthy that when the de Gaulle's had to move for the missions entrusted to Charles, the eldest children would go to boarding school, while 'la petite Anne' would always move with her parents.

Even when the war was at its height, Charles seems to have been concerned about his family, especially Anne (145–148). As the danger of war grew, he wrote a letter to his wife advising her to move to the Loiret with Anne, to live there with his sister. Later in the war, to ensure Anne's safety and education, he also asks his son to leave Paris with his sister (where they are at boarding school) and go with their mother to live with their aunt.

The actions and choices of such an important and busy father as Charles de Gaulle can of course only be understood if we look at his partner, Yvonne. Frederique Neau-Dufour's book Yvonne de Gaulle gives us a good picture of how Yvonne got on with her children, especially Anne. This makes it easier to link her to Charles' life and decisions.

From the first descriptions of Yvonne's life with her youngest child, Anne, we see that her husband Charles played a crucial role. It was he who ensured that the family showed a deep humanity in bringing up their daughter, despite all their worries.

Anne's birth shocked the mother even more than the father. One before Anne and one after, Yvonne's life is like a broken line. In the end, she finds a powerful ally in her husband. Remarkably human, Charles is the right man for the job. His concern for Yvonne, his refusal to blame her for anything, and his immediate love for little Anne are priceless balm for his wife. Instead of rejecting her and pushing her aside, instead of being ashamed of her, he shows her an abundance of love. The behavior of her husband is crucial to Yvonne. Charles shows her the way. He shows her that there is another way of looking at things, beyond the worries that Anne provokes, beyond the contingencies. Anne's father expresses touching affection for her. He, so modest and reserved, had no hesitation in giving her kisses and taking her in his arms. He hugged her, told her stories, tried to put things between her fingers, objects, handkerchiefs, made her clap, sang nursery rhymes despite her shaky voice.

The de Gaulles showed an impressive strength of character. Henceforth, they would do whatever it took to enable Anne to lead a normal life within the family. Here, whatever the conditions, they gave her all the medical and emotional care possible. As long as she lived, they would keep this promise, which was highly original for that time.

Anne's death in early 1948 was a great loss for Charles and his wife. Anne was buried in the simple cemetery at Colombey, where Charles and his wife would later be laid to rest. Anne's life and death were the inspiration and motivation for Yvonne's creation of the Foundation. With Charles's discreet support and advice, Yvonne created the Foundation Anne de Gaulle (fondation-anne-de-gaulle.org/). The values that Yvonne put at the heart of the foundation are still valid today. They ensured that a 'different' approach was taken compared to the asylums of the time. For example, they wanted to create a friendly environment for young women with intellectual disabilities. From the very beginning, they believed in the potential for development of the women—they wanted to do more than just to house them. They also wanted to be open to women from poorer families. It has always been the foundation's intention to be close to and in the community.

3.2 How Would a World-Famous Philosopher-Psychologist-Educator Embrace His Role as a Father? John Dewey

John Dewey is a name that rings a bell. He is considered to be one of the greatest American philosophers of the twentieth century.

As a professor at the University of Chicago, he had a chair with a very wide range of subjects. This allowed him to research and publish in the field of philosophy: he developed very fascinating insights into 'democracy', for example, in the field of psychology: he argued, among other things, that ideas are primarily tools that people use to solve problems in the environment in which they find themselves. (In doing so, he reacted sharply to the strong belief in S-R-C strings that prevailed at the time.) And in the field of pedagogy, this allowed him to further develop his ideas at the Laboratory School in Chicago. He was against traditional education which placed children in a very passive/reproductive role. He was in favor of children having experiences and being very active in the world. He sought the ideal balance between an experiential/thematic approach on the one hand, and a knowledge-based approach on the other, which he gave a place in the curriculum through subject teachers. He also saw schools as miniature democracies where children learned to balance needs and wants. His thinking about learning and education, and his philosophical musings about a democratic society, showed that he saw all the elements of his broad field as closely interrelated.

What few people seem to know—but what we were able to learn thanks to our esteemed colleague Scott Danforth (2018)—is that Dewey and his wife adopted an Italian boy—Sabino—after losing two of their own children.

From the writings of Danforth (who draws on the work of Jay Martin, one of Dewey's most important biographers), we learn that John Dewey and his wife were very consistent in their approach to their adopted physically handicapped son.

The Dewey's met Sabino in Venice in 1905. The boy was 8 years old at the time. Back then, they were living with great grief, having lost two children. In addition, the University of Chicago had merged Dewey's Laboratory School with another school, so the couple had a lot to worry about. This prompted Dewey to leave and accept a position at Columbia University in New York.

They talked to Sabino's mother, who handed over her son, hoping that he could have a better life with his new rich American parents.

Few texts on Dewey include impairment or Sabino as interesting enough to warrant attention, and yet it must not have been an easy task (even for wealthy American intellectuals) to raise a child at a time when 'disability' was a highly stigmatized phenomenon.

Danforth took on the challenge of providing an additional historical analysis to help us better understand what the upbringing of this child might have meant for the family, and for Dewey in particular, at a time when eugenics was emerging.

Sabino's arrival in New York from Europe was a matter of great urgency, partly because the boy needed treatment for tuberculosis in his knee.

This led to major orthopedic surgery followed by months of immobilization. The little boy lived in pain day and night, and then John Dewey and his wife turned out to be very patient and comforting parents, telling stories, and caring for the little boy, especially on nights filled with pain.

It turned out that the boy would have to live with pain and limited mobility for several years after this operation. His knee would hinder him for the rest of his life, but he would grow into an active and athletic young man.

This positive story of growing up is taking place in a society where both TB and physical disability are surrounded by a wide range of cultural beliefs. We know from stigma research that this cannot be separated from people's fears on the one hand and social developments on the other. (Here: in the example of Sabino, the advance of industrialization.)

In Sabino's lifetime, the Deweys were also faced with the development of eugenics (Bashford & Levine, 2010) in the United States. Both TB and disability were then seen as hereditary phenomena that manifested themselves in families. What's more, in a country then overrun with immigrants, the fear of TB spreading rapidly was palpable. Worldwide, TB patients were isolated and treated in special sanatoria far from civilization in 'clean air' areas.

With publications on the 'Kallikak family' (Lombardo, 2008), for example, the leaders of the new 'science' of eugenics launched ideas for the elimination (read: institutionalization/read: denial of access to public schools) of 'inferior human beings' and for compulsory, controlled sterilization programs to be carried out on 'these' families. They came to be seen as representing 'intergenerational inferiority'.

John Dewey and his wife were committed to inclusion 'avant la lettre' with their son. At no point did the Deweys subscribe to the then-current idea that children like Sabino were incapable of learning. With the help of her husband's extensive social network, Alice was a strong advocate for Sabino's inclusion in a mainstream school throughout his school career. This was not something that could be taken for granted: the little boy came from Italy and therefore had a language problem as far as the English language was concerned. In addition, the presence in a mainstream school of a person with tuberculosis (remember the fear of tuberculosis) and a disability (remember the rise of eugenics) was clearly seen as atypical. Finally, Sabino's schooling seemed to be regularly interrupted by moments when he had to stay at home because of too much pain.

In complete accordance with his pedagogical views (let us remember that Dewey was a firm believer in the interests of children and believed that real-life activities should be organized at school), father John went to the school to plead for Sabino to follow his own trajectory in terms of technical skills. In fact, it turned out that the boy was technically gifted: he could drive a car quickly and thus became the chauffeur for many members of the family. He also liked to tinker with the car and was very good at it. The family farm gave him particular satisfaction, with lots to maintain and fix.

As they searched for 'a good school' and 'a good curriculum' for their son, the Dewey's remained very aware that the schools they approached were not used to having children with disabilities. The Deweys also remained very critical of how the school continued to monitor not only the academic, but also the social and emotional aspects of their son's curriculum.

John and his wife put a lot of energy into motivating Sabino to take up his opportunities in higher education. Despite several attempts, the young man had not been able to gain a degree.

It is fascinating to get to know John Dewey as the father of an adopted son with a disability. But did this situation have an effect on his thinking and social action? Danforth dares to doubt, simply because Dewey and his wife never referred directly to Sabino or publicly included disability as an important factor in their analysis and public discussions. It seems to have remained largely a private matter. (To get things done for Sabino, they clearly used Dewey's large social network.) This does not change the fact that Dewey and his wife never missed an opportunity to advocate Sabino's full participation in society. (Their quest for inclusive education for their son is quite remarkable for that time.)

And yet, it could be that Dewey's tireless commitment to the 'disadvantaged' was strongly influenced by his son's constant confrontation with the threat of exclusion. Dewey (especially after he moved to New York) took an increasingly outspoken stance against racism and the oppression of women.

And yet, it may be that Dewey's fierce opposition to instrumentalizing psychology through intelligence testing was partly shaped by living with Sabino. As early as 1922, Dewey wrote of his concern that testing and then classifying people could divert educators from believing in and working with children's individual talents and interests. In this view, Dewey was already very close to the opposition to the all-important medical-individual model that would be waged much later by disability studies activists and academics.

References

Bashford, A., & Levine, P. (Eds.). (2010). *The Oxford handbook of the history of eugenics*. Oxford University Press.

Clerc, C. (2000). *Les de Gaulle*. Une famille française, Paris, Editions Nil, ISBN: 978-2841111534

Danforth, S. (2018). Disability in the family: John and Alice Dewey raising their son, Sabino. *Teachers College Record, 120*(2), 1–30. https://doi.org/10.1177/016146811812000203

Lombardo, P. (2008). *Three generations, no imbeciles*. The Johns Hopkins University Press.

Neau-Dufour, F. (2010). *Yvonne de Gaulle*. Paris, Fayard, 585, ISBN: 978-2213627502

4

Fathers of Children with Disabilities/ Artists Who Have Contributed Very Actively to Disability Studies as a Field

Abstract This chapter describes the impact that fathers of children with disabilities can have through their creative work as artists. Michael Bérubé, Gusti, Pierre Mertens, and Dan Habib are advocates for their children and for people with disabilities, using their artistic talents as writers, illustrators/storytellers, and documentary filmmakers.

In keeping with the ideas of Disability Studies in Education, our four artists provide us with deep and rich accounts of their lives with the children. Their personal narratives are combined with social criticism. This ensures that 'rusty' stereotypes are challenged and values such as inclusion and respect are promoted.

Keywords Advocacy • Fatherhood • Inclusion • Creativity • Resilience • Literature • Documentary • Graphic arts

With two particularly meticulously described books about/with his son, Michael Bérubé tries to provoke greater understanding of his son and family life on the one hand. On the other hand, with the stories in his books, he also wants to call for social justice—with this, Bérubé clearly

G. Van Hove, *Fathering Children with Disabilities*,
https://doi.org/10.1007/978-3-031-82960-4_4

positions himself within a Disability Studies framework. He makes a plea not to ignore or avoid his son because of his disability, but to give him a place in the world by regarding him as a human being (Kirby, 2013).

Bérubé can be seen as an incredibly talented (self-)observer and descriptor; we would like to illustrate this with two excerpts, one from each book.

The book 'Life as we know it. A father, a family and an exceptional child' (1998) by Michael Bérubé[1] had a far-reaching effect on us as long ago, and contains extremely valuable small stories that demonstrate that as a father, Bérubé did have a very close relationship and close physical contact with his child and wanted to work with his partner for the good of that child. Let us share just one marvelous fragment from Bérubé's book:

> *…Then late one weird night after his first week or two of tubelessness, Jamie spoke to us for the first time. It was 2 or 3 a.m; and I was watching The Abyss on the VCR while holding a bottle which Jamie was drinking with great deliberation. I don't remember the movie too well, but I do remember holding a half-full bottle to the light and thinking, at this rate he'll finish this sometime around dawn, when suddenly I heard an eerie little wail. I assumed it had come from the TV, but when I looked down I saw my two-month-old Jamie nestled in the crook of my elbow, all tensed up, staring at me with wide, wide eyes and trying to speak: "ooooooo", he was saying in a thready, raspy voice. "Ooooooo". Janet asleep next to me on the couch, woke up in alarm. "What was that?" she asked. "That was him" I said with a jog of the elbow. "I think he is oooooo-ing". "Is he hurt? He sounds like he's hurt". Up to this point even Jamie's cries had been soundless, thanks in part to his floppy larynx and his shallow breathing. 'I don't know' I replied. The oooooo-ing went on, every bit as eerie and unsettling as when started.… But after a few minutes his efforts – and particularly his expressions – were unmistakable: he was saying hello to us, and when I said hello back, he started to smile. He wanted to make something of an opening statement. His muscles weren't ready to pull it off, but his spirit was strong and clear. He was home, in the arms of his proud but profoundly sleepy parents, and he wanted to let them know that he knew it.…* (1998, 93–94)

The first connection with a child the child labelled as disabled, with a lot of challenges already at the very start and his father who is worried

[1] Bérubé is the Edwin Erle Sparks Professor of Literature at Penn State University. The book was nominated as a New York Times Notable Book of the Year.

and who does not always recognize what is needed or how the baby can be read, but who is close and open to get to know his son. The child that needs a lot of (professional) care becomes slowly the son of his father and mother and is at home after spending a long time in hospital. Every parent of children with labels can remember those decisive moments.

The second book, too, is full of very rich miniatures that help draw out an increasingly beautiful father–son relationship.

> *...It was his last season at the day care before he started kindergarten, and the occasion was a classroom game in which the children told their teachers what they wanted to be when they grew up. From every child, except Jaimie, the list of occupations bore out the joke that if we'd all grown up to be what we said we wanted to be at the age of five, we'd live in a world populated by cowboys, firefighters, and ballerinas. When the class got to Jaimie, though, the teachers weren't even sure that he would understand the question, let alone come up with an intelligible answer. Still, they politely asked him, last among the preschool kids. 'And what would you like to be when you grow up Jaimie?' Later that day, Janet and I were told that Jaimie had answered the question immediately, and with just one word. Big....* (2016, 19–20)

And with growing up comes all sorts of extra challenges that cause Bérubé (like many parents) a lot of anxiety, that anxiety that contributes to letting go of a child

> *...The weekend was complicated, Janet was attending a funeral, and I was attending a class reunion. Jamie was with Trevor (his nephew, a young man with mild cerebral palsy and probably dixit Bérubé residing somewhere in the autism spectrum). On Thursday night they texted us a picture of themselves in the bleachers at Yankee Stadium. 'How nice' I thought, 'Bud (Trevor's father) took the boys to a game and took a picture of them'. But I was wrong. They took themselves to the Stadium and took a selfie. When they got back home from the game around 11 p.m., they took themselves out for sushi....* (2016, 14)

These are delightful descriptions in which, on the one hand, there is a lot of concern, but on the other hand, Bérubé grows enormously proud that his son has become: big.

Besides the detailed descriptions, Bérubé's work offers many openings to argue for 'the world as a more welcoming place' (2016, 171). In doing so, he pays a lot of attention to the question of when and how far we can and want to intervene genetically. In doing so, he puts on the table the very important (for him and his family situation) question of whether the life Jaimie lives might then be worth less than the lives of supposedly 'normal' people? He also asks where 'normality' begins or ends (and who in turn decides that?) (2016, 181).

In a long search for answers to these very complex questions—knowing that Jaimie is there and is living a happy life—Bérubé finds temporary solace in email exchanges with Tom Shakespeare. The latter states (2016, 184): '… my messy, possible incoherent position is that we should accept a measure of diversity and difference, because human frailty is unavoidable, but that where the balance tips into suffering and restriction we should do whatever we can do to avoid it. While still valuing, supporting, and including all those individuals who end up, despite our efforts, with profound disability…'.

With these questions, Bérubé clearly positions himself within the Disability Studies research field where the questions Bérubé raises here remain the basic questions to this day. The very title of one of Prof Dan Goodley's latest works, 'Disability and Other Human Questions' (2020), refers in this context to Bérubé's quest. Goodley also draws on decades of research to argue that disability has much to offer when we contemplate what it means to be human in the twenty-first century. He addresses questions such as 'who's allowed to be human?'; 'are human beings dependent?'; and 'what does it mean to be human in the digital age?'

As we said before, some very talented fathers manage to take us playfully and creatively through their quest for the meaning of being a father of a child with a disability.

A great example is graphic artist GUSTI (2021) (real name: Gustavo Ariel Rosemfett Abramovic), an Argentine illustrator. He launched the book Mallko (2017), a book in which he shows the emotions he has gone through as the father of a child with Down Syndrome (disappointment, anger and sadness; but also joy and love).

In the book, it is particularly striking how the father learns to deal with his son (and his feelings toward him) primarily by looking at others. He sees how his wife, Mallko's mother, very naturally senses how best to deal with the child. Or he observes his other son take on the role of big brother with great elegance. Or he watches how little girls, the friends of Mallko, soon turn out to see how good this little boy is at 'love-giving'. His friends to encourage Gusti to see his son 'as he is' and learn to enjoy him.

Gradually, Gusti discovers that Mallko is a very playful child and let playing and fantasy be the point where son and father easily find each other.

In a playful, non-sugar-sweet way, this book provides basic information about Down Syndrome, but especially Mallko's family and Gusti's fatherhood are beautifully illustrated through drawings, poems, texts. This book did not win the 2016 Bologna Ragazzi Award (in the Disability category) by coincidence.

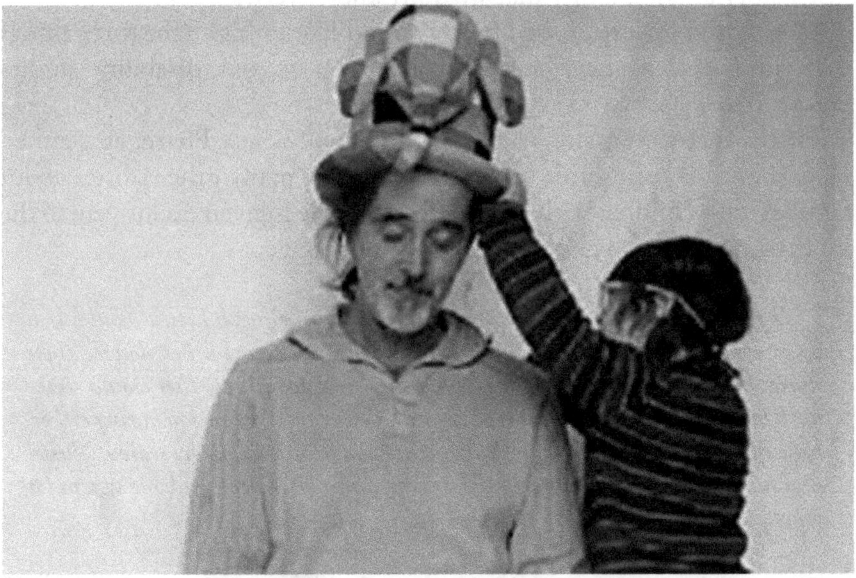

Pierre Mertens is a Belgian visual artist and psychotherapist. Shortly after the birth of his eldest daughter Liesje, who was born with spina bifida, he and his partner started a self-help group for people with spina bifida and their families. Pierre was the driving force behind specialist referral centers in Belgium for children with spina bifida. He is—now that spina bifida has almost disappeared in The North—as president of Child Help, on the ground every day to assist families in The South and their children with spina bifida with the knowledge and techniques developed in The North, some of which are proving to be affordable and implementable in The South.

After Liesje's death at the age of 11, Mertens and his partner were confused for a while. Pierre tried to pay tribute to his daughter and his family by writing a book in which he tries to find words for the confusing and intense life of his daughter.

This book gives us an unprecedented insight into the life, feelings, and actions of the father of a disabled child. Do we learn so much about Pierre's feelings because he is a psychotherapist? Or is it because he is an artist that we are able to see so many different layers of who he is? Or is it just a story about a father that we don't know (yet)?

In my brief review of the book, I would like to highlight three things that, in my view, have a clear connection to our disability studies perspective.

Firstly, there are many passages in the book where Pierre, as a father, talks about his caring role for his daughter. In many other stories about families with children with disabilities, this role is given exclusively to the mother. Allow me to give you my favorite passage:

> *… The staff knew us because I used to go to the scanner with Lies. I would then be given a lead apron, and I would tell her stories to calm her down. These stories had to be a bit boring, because if they were too funny, Lies would shake with laughter while she had to lie very still. They could not be too boring either, because then Liesje would not be distracted enough and might get scared. Nurses and radiologists have listened to these stories through the microphone system for years….* (p. 133)

Pierre is also a master in the forging of alliances with people who will have a special role for his daughter, his wife, and himself. He seeks strategic partnerships, I'll let him explain. '*You learn to choose your partners, you take the others and let them play their power game. As long as they act medically correct…*' (p. 123). And so, at the beginning of his little daughter's life, he manages to enter into a special relationship with a nun who works as a nurse in the premature baby ward. '*We got to know Sister Celestine better and she suggested that we visit Liesje outside visiting hours. The sister carefully laid Liesje on the nursing cushion and unfolded the blanket. She talks to Liesje all the time. We appreciate this.... The nurse wants to give Liesje to my wife, but she pushes me forward, uncertain. I take Liesje as the nurse explains: with one hand I support her head, with the other I support her bottom. In the lukewarm water she ceased to cry. My wife gently splashes water on her....*' (pp. 61–62). For Pierre and his wife, Sister Celestine was a beacon of light during the first uncertain weeks of their daughter's life. It seemed to them that she was living in that ward. Later in Liesje's life, a life that often takes place in hospitals and doctors' rooms, Pierre learns to appreciate the work of Richard, the transvestite nurse. He forms a special bond with Liesje and her parents. Even when things go completely wrong and Liesje is living her last days, Richard remains at the side of the parents. '... *Only Richard still talks to us. He explains to Liesje over and over again which syringe he is putting where and why. He says "Hi Liesje" when he comes in and "Bye Liesje" when he leaves. He discreetly shares our hope, our despair, without adding an ounce of himself. He is close without going away. He is with us and that is all we can bear. This is consolation, as Liesje does...*' (p. 139). Pierre experiences with Richard what Mia Mingus has called 'access intimacy': access intimacy is that hard to describe feeling when someone else 'gets' your access needs (Mingus, https://leavingevidence.wordpress.com/2011/05/05/access-intimacy-the-missing-link/).

Finally, Pierre also emerges as an activist and 'gentle anarchist'. Coming from a hippy era where many hierarchical relationships were questioned, he learned to scan and fathom the medical and health landscape. Together with his wife, he set up a support group for parents of children with spina bifida (later joined by adults with spina bifida), he organized congresses that led to Europe-wide discussions on ethical issues such as euthanasia, he and others drew up 'survival tips' for dealing with doctors, he campaigned for inclusive education and deinstitutionalization, he later also began to work with groups of parents and experts with experience of spina bifida on other continents. He does all this with an incredible drive and visionary approach, harmonizing this aspect with emotions and focusing on small things:

> …*When I talk about you, my voice still shakes and tears come to my eyes. These are not tears of sadness, but of joy, because I feel that you are still with me. On my chair is still the sheepskin on which you sat in your wheelchair. I keep restoring it because I don't want to part with it. For me, you live on in this great group of young people and adults with spina bifida in Africa who have been given a fair start in life through Child-Help. Every time one of them sends me a WhatsApp message, I wink at the picture I made of you and say: we did it again. You and me. They're just words, but they do so much good….* (p. 158)

Some fathers write, others draw; you also have some who photograph and film. One such filmmaker-father of a son with disabilities is Dan Habib. He developed several Award-winning documentaries; most of these films are used to advocate for the inclusion of people with disabilities. In these documentaries, Habib puts human rights at the center.

In collaboration with the University of New Hampshire, Habib made the documentary 'Including Samuel', and in this film he introduces us to his son Samuel who has been diagnosed with cerebral palsy. The Habib family makes every effort to include Samuel in all aspects of life: the family activities per se, going to school in a regular school, enjoying sports in a sports club, participating in the scouting movement, playing together with nieces and nephews. Besides all these actions, the documentary also shows that many doctor's visits and hospitalizations exhaust the family and don't just let all the days pass in rosy light. Dan Habib films much of the footage, but also appears on screen himself as a passionate father who explores possibilities that allow his son to have a good life. The many beautiful moments in the film are also interspersed with moments when the father (parents) themselves are at a loss as to how to handle certain situations, or almost feel guilty because their other son also needs attention (and gets).

So many years later—we are writing in 2022—Habib is releasing a new documentary in which his son Samuel is once again the main character. As with Bérubé in his second book, Habib involves Samuel much more as a co-filmmaker in the second film. Samuel starts from the point of view that people with disabilities more than others are too uninformed to make the transition from childhood/school to adult life.

To look into the future, he visits several Disability Rights activists whom he sees as mentors. He puts questions to them about attitudes toward them, the expectations others have for them, how they have dealt with the transition themselves, and with some he discusses sexuality and relationships. Samuel manages to meet not the least of these. We think of Judith Heumann, Maysoon Zayid, Bob Williams, and Keith Jones, among others.

In the film, we also see that—unlike the documentary 'Including Samuel'—Samuel is now no longer only supported by family, but also receives professional personal assistance. The collaboration with his father as co-director is nicely portrayed in moments that he prepares interview questions together for the mentors he will visit. In addition, Dan Habib as father also continues to address people when they make derogatory statements about Samuel. In the documentary, Samuel also explores presidential candidates and their plans regarding persons with disabilities during election time. This leads to an odd encounter with (now) President Biden who starts stroking Samuels' cheek while talking to him.

Dan Habib is a father who uses his exceptional talent for the good of his child (and by extension, in other documentaries, for other people with disabilities). He manages to show behind and in front of the camera that as a father he is very committed to his son's life and well-being, that he, together with Samuel's mother and brother, can create a family environment that allows Samuel to flourish as much as possible, as well as using Samuel's very specific situation to reflect more broadly on human rights and disability. This is a father who was not to be missed in this book.

The three father-artists bring layers of stories about the upbringing of their children with disabilities that really take us to the heart of the relationship between father and child. The three fathers also manage to take an activist stance on behalf of their children and lead a fight for a respectful place for children with disabilities in society.

References

Bérubé, M. (1998). *Life as we know it: A father, a family, and an exceptional child.* Vintage Books.

Bérubé, M. (2016). *Life as Jamie knows it: An exceptional child grows up.* Beacon Press.

Goodley, D. (2020). *Disability and Other Human Questions*. Emerald Publishing, Leeds, 145p., ISBN: 978-1839827075

Gusti. (2017). *Mallko* (trans. version in Dutch). Memphis Belle.

Gusti. (2021). Gusti (Gustavo Ariel Rosemffet Abramovich) Illustrator–Argentina. *Bookbird: A Journal of International Children's Literature, 59*(4), 2. https://doi.org/10.1353/bkb.2021.0048

Habib, D. (Director). (2009). *Including Samuel*. https://includingsamuel.com/

Habib, D. (Director). (2022). *My Disability Roadmap*. https://likerightnow-films.com/film/3356/My-Disability-Roadmap

Kirby, C. (2013). *Meeting disability with resiliency, hope, and agency: A narrative study of caregivers of children with cognitive and physical disabilities* (Doctoral dissertation, University of North Carolina at Greensboro, Greensboro, NC.

Mertens, P. (2024). *Liesje. Zoeken naar woorden voor de geboorte en de dood van een bijzonder kind (Liesje. A search for words to mark the birth and death of a very special child)*. (New ed). Pelckmans.

5

Suppose We Listen to Fathers of Children with Disabilities: Our Own Little Research Project

Abstract This chapter aims to explore and document the experiences and contributions of fathers who are actively involved in the care of their disabled children. Six fathers shared their stories and experiences in detail. The research material was analyzed using Jackson and Mazzei's 'thinking with theory' approach. The findings show that fathers are indeed 'becoming fathers' (Braidotti), challenging traditional gender stereotypes of caregiving; they seem to be able to adapt and reorganize their embodied habitus (Doucet) to meet the unique needs of their children. An extremely important theme in the fathers' stories is the emphasis on 'togetherness'; shared activities open opportunities for fathers and children to develop and grow. This study highlights the importance of fathers in families with disabled children. They can contribute to the caregiving process and thus redefine the role of a 'good father': they show responsibility, and they invest in a sensitive and responsive relational care.

This chapter is an expanded version of a presentation I had the pleasure of giving with my colleague Prof. Elisabeth De Schauwer at the AERA conference in Chicago, 2023.

G. Van Hove, *Fathering Children with Disabilities*,
https://doi.org/10.1007/978-3-031-82960-4_5

Keywords Conversations • Thinking with theory • Good father • Responsibility • Other cultures • Becoming • Caring masculinities • Ethics of care • Listening • Together

5.1 Introduction

In the past, literature concerning families with disabled children mainly approached and investigated family perspectives, in collaboration with mothers. Fathers were not involved (Bogossian et al., 2019; Pleck, 2012). They were described as 'absent', 'seeking refuge in their work', as 'someone who mainly does nice and playful things with the children, while the task of providing care is left to the mother'. Some authors refer to a 'deficit perspective' of men in families with a disabled child (Brotherson et al., 2005).

While supporting families, we met fathers[1] who are doing their best to step out of their partner's shadow. They told us that during meetings

---

[1] We would like to emphasize in this footnote that the fathers that we have had the opportunity to meet in this small study do not include any fathers from 'other cultures'. This is a major omission, and one that we are certainly going to address in the concluding chapter. Some will ask: are these fathers not there? Of course they are, we had the opportunity to meet them indirectly when our Spanish, Italian, Greek, Indian, Brazilian, German, and Congolese student members of our Erasmus student exchanges did interviews with fathers in their countries. In view of the sensitive nature of these interviews, we then decided not to include them in our research reports.

In the production of this book, we were faced with a choice: if fathers from 'other cultures' do not appear in our own research, should we write a separate chapter about them? After consultation with the publisher, and in the hope of not setting these fathers apart, it was decided not to do this.

And of course, we are aware of many colleagues that do write about these fathers (but then they often confine themselves to just these fathers). A few examples are given below.

Through Dr Femke Bannink Mbazzi, we met a Ugandan father who loved and cared for his disabled son. You can follow this story in a video report: https://www.ugent.be/pp/orthopedagogiek/en/research/ongoingresarch/obuntubulamu.htm.

In 2018, a doctoral dissertation by Shannon Burns-Darden entitled 'African American fathers raising an autistic child' was submitted to the accredited online Walden University (USA).

We also know that colleagues have completed a research project with fathers in Japan. You can read about this in: Sato N, Araki A. (2022). Fathers' involvement in raising children with severe mental retardation and multiple disabilities. *Journal of Family Nursing*, 28(1): 57–68. https://doi.org/10.1177/10748407211037345.

In the Middle East, too, we are seeing the first research articles appearing, as an example of which we refer to: Ahmed Mohamed, Maxwell Peprah Opoku, Shamsa Almarzooqi, J-F, Haseena Shah. (2024). Nationwide study of fathers' involvement in the rehabilitation of children with disabilities in the United Arab Emirates, *Heliyon, 10*(10). https://doi.org/10.1016/j.heliyon.2024.e30980.

no-one looked in their direction. The recommendations of experts were formulated 'for the mother' (Mueller & Buckley, 2014a, 2014b). 'I just sat there as if I was the chauffeur' dixit a father.

But there are signs that changes are taking place. More articles and chapters can be found, which bring in the situation of fathers with disabled children (Bonsall, 2014a, 2014b, 2015, 2018; Boström & Broberg, 2014; Boyd et al., 2019; Boyraz & Sayger, 2011; Cameron & Cooper, 2021; Carpenter & Towers, 2008; Davys et al., 2017; Dollahite & Hawkins, 1998; Flippin & Crais, 2011; Marshak et al., 2019; Mavrogianni & Lampropoulou, 2020; Mitchell & Lashewicz, 2015, 2018, 2019; MacDonald & Hastings, 2010; Marsh et al., 2018, 2020; Rivard & Mastel-Smith, 2014; Scorgie et al., 2004; Singh, 2019; Wright et al., 2016; Yoong & Koritsas, 2012). These signs prove that many colleagues are of the opinion that 'fathers matter'.

5.2 Becoming Fathers

Andrea Doucet provided fascinating insights to shine a light on fathers as living in an assemblage (Hickey-Moody, 2019). Doucet (2013, 284) states that: 'One critical missing link within our understandings of gender differences in care work is that of male embodiment in care giving'. Fathers and mothers cannot be seen as simply interchangeable disembodied subjects. Doucet borrows the concept of 'embodied habitus' from Bourdieu: boys learn that the primary purpose of their bodies is to perform physical (masculine) activities and that boys who become fathers play with children using a body that has predominantly learned to be sporting, take risks, and to be emotionally independent. She asserts that fathers and mothers are embodied subjects and that 'bodies matter'. These bodies are in a constant 'state of flux' (p. 299) given the multiplicity of voices (Mazzei, 2016) that surround them and give rise to considerable tension and contradictions.

In this chapter, we meet the challenge to look at this 'state of flux', this 'becoming-fathers' (Braidotti, 2002). First, we listened carefully to fathers. In the analysis we looked for small cracks in stereotypical images spread about fathers. We explore the question: what can we learn from fathers who do not conform to the archetype?

5.3 Methodology

We rely on long conversations with 6 Flemish fathers (Information in Table 5.1).

We invited fathers who had a child with a label to tell their story. They were asked to seek out photos or video clips that could make it easier to talk about their fatherhood. We followed Sermijn et al. (2009, p. 17), whose starting point was: 'The intention is that you tell us what you find important'. The conversations did not fulfil the characteristics of a nicely composed linear whole. Instead, we received an amalgam of ideas, memories, feelings, and events (Sermijn et al., 2009, p. 18). What we heard were testimonies with non-linear timelines and relationships between causes and results lacked clarity.

The analysis of the interviews is based on Jackson and Mazzei's (2013) 'thinking with theory'. Theory and concepts play a vital role in their working with data. They make use of Deleuze and Guattari's (1987) 'plugging in': data are read with theory and the theory is read with the data.

Our primary aim was to work with the concept of 'embodied and relational care'. In the analysis we paid particular attention to 'miniatures', in which fathers refer to moments when they came into confrontation with their 'embodied habitus', when they have been challenged to expand their repertoire of activities.

Table 5.1 Information about fathers-participants

Age father	children	Age child with label	Medical diagnosis children	Marital status	Job
48	2	15	Asperger+ADHD	Married	Engineer
43	3	11	Down Syndrome+ASS	Divorced	Teacher
38	2	13	ASS	Divorced	Workman
63	2	34	Fragile X Syndrome	Married	Retired
58	2	19	Mild Intellectual Disability + DCD+CVI	Married	Workman
39	4	10	High sensitivity	Married	Welder

5.4 Results

5.4.1 Disability Enters the Family: Effects on Tasks Fathers Perform

When talking about the tasks performed by fathers, it became obvious that several fathers—most of them after a period of adjustment—do not restrict themselves to tasks typically performed by fathers. A broad palette is presented in the accounts:

> *... I don't want other people to think 'What does he look like?'... In the past, disabled children were dressed in laughable clothes... so I take extra care to make sure he's well dressed...*
>
> *... I also talk to him about some of the 'difficulties of love'. I tell him that you can't just say 'I love you'... That has consequences and creates expectations in the other person...*
>
> *... I focus more on the psychological side ... good advice, pats on the back, but also deep discussions...*
>
> *...Yes, feeding our daughter was my job....*

And yet... one of the fathers (honestly) expressed his disillusionment at the fact that he is not able to experience what it's like to take part in 'manly activities' with his son.

> *...I like soccer and hoped that after my son was born, we would be able to kick a ball around together,... but he's not interested in that whatsoever... But there is hope... I have a grandson and I hope he will end up being bitten by the soccer bug....*

5.4.2 Together: Fathers in Connection

If we quote one word that came up in most conversations, it is: 'together'. Some of the fathers spoke of how they are constantly seeking to do those things with their child that they both passionately enjoy doing.

... like e.g., programming the computer together enjoying a shared passion for technology....

Doing things together provides fathers with opportunities to work to develop their children's strengths. This way of working together also leads to 'skill development' in the fathers themselves.

... We play music together, which helps me as it gives me the chance to play more rock, because on my own, I would stick to the blues as it's in my fingers more,....

Another father said:... *We are 'learning buddies'; you won't believe the things I've learned at times when I'm being there for my daughter and household jobs need to be done....*

For some fathers, 'together' also means 'close physical contact'

... Look at this as a typical picture showing how I approached things when she was little... I was there for her, sat her on my lap, gave her calmness, after which you saw that smile that can be seen on this photo.... It's a smile that she only had when she calmed down.... It meant that all was well....

Some fathers also spoke of the literal embodiment that forms part of their child's upbringing. *On that point we got* a detailed description of how a father uses his body during conflicts.

... I asked him to do something, but he refused and the more I asked him, the angrier he got. So, I said, 'Just stand up straight—that's all that I ask'...He stood up straight, angry, with his arms stretched out beside him and his face dropped. I went up to him and gave him a cuddle. He completely broke down in tears. He cried for 5 minutes and said sorry ...I said that I wouldn't punish him or shout at him. I said that I understood what was going on and that we didn't need to have an argument....

5.4.3 Becoming a 'Good' Father?

It is clear that these fathers were permanently searching for the 'form' of fatherhood that best suits the upbringing of their children. During the conversations, they were looking for an answer to the question: In what way do I want or am I able to fulfil the role of 'a good father'?

One of the fathers started out by saying that having a child with a disability has made him stronger. Fathers take response-ability (ability to respond) for 'what matters and what is excluded from mattering' (Barad, 2007, p. 394) and often reorient activities in the range of abilities and interests of their child. What feels precious in their life becomes very colored by the way of living of a child who wants to participate in the daily life of the family but also encounters many barriers ...

> *You must make the best of things. Living up to your responsibility... I feel more of a dad... I respond much more to him... We go out walking with our dog and I get to see my son walking with his boots on. These are very simple things that give a good feeling inside... things that make me happy... That child is happy, I am happy, the dog is happy....*

One of the other fathers spoke about his difficult search for a way in which to fulfil the ideal of 'good fatherhood'. Letting go is a very important lesson.

> *In the past, I was always striving for perfection, but I don't do that anymore: what I have learned is that perfect doesn't exist....*

Finally, we would like to recall one of the fathers, who regards fulfilling his role as a father as a learning process. Fatherhood is a matter of becoming; you are not able to think in advance what it will bring you. The disabled child is the yardstick in how fatherhood is viewed and evaluated.

> *There are always things and events that led me to reflect... I know that I am a figure of protection and that the difference between protecting and overprotecting is a small one... what I want to do is to provide my child with all of the love, understanding and structure that she needs; I would genuinely devote 200% of my effort to her... but what I also have to do the whole time is make sure that I don't forget about my other daughter....*

5.5 Discussion

5.5.1 Good Fathers

The primary outcome from the analysis of conversations about what could be regarded as a 'good father' and from the many doubts that the fathers shared with us is the insight that fatherhood is an ongoing, complex journey of discovery.

The fathers feel a strong sense of response-ability (Barad, 2007) for their children and therefore take many tasks upon themselves. These tasks consist of a wonderful mixture intending to underpin their children's strengths, whether these involve taking care of the children, focusing intensively on the relationship and the bond with the children, or thinking about and supporting plans.

The testimonies granted us an insight into their lives, governed by a great many forces, attempts to adjust and/or respond, to be more flexible. 'Fatherhood' is not a static process, but an intense and dynamic one that is experienced in the world together with the children, as a process of 'becoming-with' (Wright, 2014). This is a process that begins and proceeds by recognizing what is important to the children and therefore sets forces in motion. The latter point links nicely to Braidotti's (2002) definition of 'becoming': it is a question of undoing the structures of domination by careful and patient re-visitations, re-adjustments, micro-changes… (p. 116).

The miniatures from our rhizomatic analysis enable us to conclude that the fathers interviewed have taken up opportunities to break through the armor-plated walls of their 'embodied habitus'. When some fathers dreamed of doing 'boys' activities' with their sons (notably soccer), they were successful in winning them over. The fathers in our group have shown that they are seizing opportunities that allow 'the different registers' of their bodies to be used occasionally.

One of the main threads running through this little study is the frequent use of the word 'together'. We try to understand this better by drawing on the insights of Stephen Darwall. (Darwall is a professor of philosophy at Yale and wrote a very interesting text on 'being with' in 2011.)

In his search for what 'being with' might be, he quickly comes to the conclusion that… (p. 6) people who are thus together or with one another are OPEN to one another and mutually aware of their mutual openness.

This observation gives us the opportunity to adjust the old image of the 'absent father' or 'disinterested father'. The fathers we spoke to are in fact involved and therefore have an 'open'—in pedagogical terms, a sensitive, leading-following (Van Goidsenhoven & De Schauwer, 2020)—attitude. They try to read their children carefully. They show great respect for their children—who seem to be masters of the philosophy of 'small things and events'. They adopt a sensitive-responsive attitude[2] to do exactly those activities with their children that they discover the children like to do. The 'reciprocity' built up over time ensures that the fathers also enjoy in/through these moments.

To further understand the fathers' situation, we follow Darwall's (2011, 10ff) explanation of what he calls 'projective empathy'. To fulfil this condition of 'being with', projective empathy, fathers have often first had to give up their 'dream child' (which children with disabilities do not fulfil because of their disability) in order to work together on their child's 'dreams' through perspective taking. The latter is often a creative re-creation of previous ideas into a new pedagogical project.

The fact that 'being together' often leads to the second function described by Darwall (2011, p. 12) as 'fellow feeling' often makes all the difference. Surely an important part of what we usually seek in being with others is some seconding or affirming of our feelings and passions and so ourselves.

After talking to fathers, this 'fellow feeling' seems to be linked to a vision and experience of KAÏROS. Fathers learn with/from their children to 'take their time', to 'live in the moment', to 'enjoy the little things that happen without being planned for'. For those fathers who once had a career, for those who 'wanted to get ahead' and saw the sky as the limit, this is quite a learning process. We have learned that fathers who succeed in this appreciation for the new, learn to see it as an added value and even start to propagate it.

[2] (Darwall, p. 7): …as central as relating is to being with others, however we should bear in mind that responsiveness to the other, especially in close personal relationships, also includes sensitivity to the other's needs for space and emotional distance.

5.5.2 'Caring masculinities'

We would like to link the image of fathers of children with disabilities that we were able to capture in our small study with the concept of 'caring masculinities' as developed within Critical Studies on Men and Masculinities (CSMM).

CSMM (Elliott, 2016, 243) defines caring masculinities as … a gender equality intervention that seeks to integrate into masculine identities values and practices of care and interdependence that are traditionally, though not inescapably, associated with women.

In this description, I think we should not underestimate the importance of 'practices'. Fathers of children with disabilities often have no choice but to engage in concrete care with their partners and to think together about professional support packages.

We have had the privilege of meeting men who, through the complexity of their lives with their partner and their children (with a label), have very rich experiences and are enjoying opportunities to grow as 'caring fathers'. They certainly do not fit (any longer) into the pigeonhole of the all-important dominant man. Messner (1997) and Kimmel (2010) (in Elliot, 2016 (p. 247)) argue that caring will 'humanize' men. It will help them to engage in more quality relationships (within and outside the family). Feeling supported and taken seriously by professionals is very important for these fathers. With this support, fathers should no longer return to the original position of the dominant man.

In this process of humanization, the fathers we spoke to discovered the complexity and multifaceted nature of caring. Elliott (2016, p. 249) writes that care can be seen as not only practical but also relational, emotional, intimate, and affective.

Fathers of children who need a lot of care will find the benefits of 'interdependence' in their journey as one of the key points within the thinking about 'caring masculinities'. They can also see that, by being closely involved with their children, they benefit from the reciprocal, emotional, and social aspects of interdependence (Elliott, 2016, p. 252).

Finally, it is also good to know that in research with fathers, Hanlon (2012, in Elliott, 2016, p. 253) was able to identify many similar perspectives of 'caring masculinities' that also featured in our conversations with fathers. Men reported that caring made them feel 'responsible', 'competent' (in caring), 'proud', 'challenged', 'joy', 'fantastic', 'happy', 'brilliant', and 'wanted', particularly—though not exclusively—in relation to caring for children....

5.5.3 The Lens of Ethics of Care

The stories told by the fathers in our study also become very interesting when we try to understand them through the lens of 'ethics of care'. Two internationally renowned colleagues are our guides in this regard.

First, we learn from Tronto as early as 1993: '...the practice of care is a political ideal...the practice of care describes the qualities that democratic citizens need to live well together in a pluralistic society...only in a just, pluralistic, democratic society can care flourish...' (pp. 161–162, in: Elliott, pp. 249–250).

The fathers show that by reorganizing their lives (as well as taking on caring responsibilities for their children) they become models for Tronto's thesis (2013, p. 27): '...once we recognize the extent of care as part of human life, it becomes impossible to think politically about freedom, equality and justice for all unless we also provide for all forms of care...to pursue democracy while taking seriously how central care is to the whole of human life requires a fundamental rethinking of questions about how we organize our lives, individually and collectively...'.

Tronto's thinking plays a big part in understanding that the care that fathers give to their children is almost always coupled with an 'activist streak'. Fathers want their children to have a good life. So, they want a good education for their children. They want their children to be seen as 'real people'. They want their children to be able to be seen, to be able to appear and participate everywhere, an inclusive life is clearly a priority. In this sense, these fathers really stand for a care that (dixit Tronto, 2013, 24) '... does not work to cover up injustices... By living with their children in this well-defined way, they are trying to counter the ever-threatening exclusion of their children...' (Tronto, 2013, p. 25).

A second guide to understanding fathers' stories is Maria Puig de la Bellacasa (see in e.g. Vandenbussche et al., 2024), which leads us to a different approach to 'listening'. The fathers in our study strive to become exceptionally good listeners who, through their active listening, do not want to simply fill the children's needs themselves.

By listening in this way, they can discover the 'uniqueness' of their children and allow them 'to shine'. These fathers no longer want their children to disappear into family foreign 'labels' or as a member of a 'target group'. Fathers we have spoken with do not simply use standard programs and solutions. There are many opportunities here to support the 'radical relationality' observed among some fathers (their children really belong, their children are given time to relate, their children lead them to discover their own competences as caregivers). Because—and this is a very personal viewpoint—professionals and local politicians can learn a lot from these fathers precisely because they are not (or do not want to be) neutral. These fathers are taking sides (for their children). These fathers show us how things can be done in a different way (from the standard way). These fathers are best seen as allies for those others (professionals, local politicians) who discover that the threat of bureaucratization and instrumentalization can be averted, and one of our options is to listen carefully to fathers who are listening to their children.

References

Barad, K. (2007). *Meeting the universe halfway: Quantum physics and the entanglement of matter and meaning*. Duke University Press. https://doi.org/10.1215/9780822388128

Bogossian, A., King, G., Lach, L. M., Currie, M., Nicholas, D., McNeill, T., & Saini, M. (2019). (Unpacking) father involvement in the context of childhood neurodisability research: A scoping review. *Disability and Rehabilitation, 41*(1), 110–124. https://doi.org/10.1080/09638288.2017.1370497

Bonsall, A. (2014a). The social context of occupations: Analysis of a father feeding his daughter diagnosed with cerebral palsy. *OTJR: Occupation, Participation and Health, 34*(4), 193–201. https://doi.org/10.3928/15394492-20141006-04

Bonsall, A. (2014b). "This is what we do": Constructing postmodern families through occupations. *Journal of Occupational Science*. https://doi.org/10.1080/14427591.2014.914459

Bonsall, A. (2015). Scenes of fathering: The automobile as a place of occupation. *Scandinavian Journal of Occupational Therapy, 22*(6), 462–469. https://doi.org/10.3109/11038128.2015.1057223

Bonsall, A. (2018). Narrative transitions in views and behaviors of fathers parenting children with disabilities. *Journal of Family Studies, 24*(2), 95–108. https://doi.org/10.1080/13229400.2015.1106336

Boström, P. K., & Broberg, M. (2014). Fathers of children with ID. *Journal of Intellectual Disability Research, 58*(9), 810–821. https://doi.org/10.1111/jir.12093

Boyd, M. J., Iacono, T., & McDonald, R. (2019). The perceptions of fathers about parenting a child with developmental disability: A scoping review. *Journal of Policy and Practice in Intellectual Disabilities, 16*, 312–324. https://doi.org/10.1111/jppi.12287

Boyraz, G., & Sayger, T. V. (2011). Psychological well-being among fathers of children with and without disabilities: The role of family cohesion, adaptability, and paternal self-efficacy. *American Journal of Men's Health*. https://doi.org/10.1177/1557988310372538

Braidotti, R. (2002). *Metamorphoses: Toward a feminist theory of becoming*. Polity Press.

Brotherson, S., Dollahite, D., & Hawkins, A. (2005). Generative fathering and the dynamics of connection between fathers and their children. *Fathering, 3*(1), 1–28.

Cameron, H., & Cooper, L. (2021). Fathers' experiences as carers for autistic children with learning disabilities. *British Journal of Learning Disabilities, 49*(1), 13–22. https://doi.org/10.1111/bld.12349

Carpenter, B., & Towers, C. (2008). Recognizing fathers: The needs of fathers of children with disabilities. *Support for Learning, 23*(3), 118–125.

Darwall, S. (2011). Being With. *The Southern Journal of Philosophy, 49*, 4–24. https://doi.org/10.1111/j.2041-6962.2011.00054.x

Davys, D., Mitchell, D., & Martin, R. (2017). Fathers of people with intellectual disability: A review of the literature. *Journal of Intellectual Disabilities, 21*(2), 175–196. https://doi.org/10.1177/1744629516650129

Deleuze, G., & Guattari, F. (1987). *A thousand plateaus* (B. Massumi, trans.). Continuum.

Dollahite, D., & Hawkins, A. (1998). A conceptual ethic of generative fathering. *The Journal of Men's Studies, 7*(1), 109–132.

Doucet, A. (2013). A "choreography of becoming": Fathering, embodied care, and new materialisms. *Canadian Review of Sociology/Revue canadienne de sociologie, 50*(3), 284–305. https://doi.org/10.1111/cars.12016

Elliott, K. (2016). Caring masculinities: Theorizing an emerging concept. *Men and Masculinities, 19*(3), 240–259. https://doi.org/10.1177/1097184X15576203

Flippin, M., & Crais, E. R. (2011). The need for more effective father involvement in early autism intervention: A systematic review and recommendations. *Journal of Early Intervention, 33*(1), 24–50. https://doi.org/10.1177/1053815111400415

Hanlon, N. (2012). *Masculinities, care and equality: Identity and nurture in men's lives*. Palgrave Macmillan.

Hickey-Moody, A. (2019). Performaty, assemblage, affect. In *Deleuze and masculinity* (pp. 29–62). Springer. https://doi.org/10.1007/978-3-030-01749-1_2

Jackson, A. Y., & Mazzei, L. M. (2013). Plugging one text into another: Thinking with theory in qualitative research. *Qualitative Inquiry, 19*(4). https://doi.org/10.1177/1077800412471510

MacDonald, E. E., & Hastings, R. P. (2010). Mindful parenting and care involvement of fathers of children with intellectual disabilities. *Journal of Child and Family Studies, 19*, 236–240. https://doi.org/10.1007/s10826-008-9243-9

Marsh, L., Brown, M., & McCann, E. (2020). The views and experiences of fathers of children with intellectual disabilities: A systematic review of the international evidence. *Journal of Policy and Practice in Intellectual Disabilities, 17*(2), 79–90. https://doi.org/10.1111/jppi.12328

Marsh, L., Warren, P.-L., & Savage, E. (2018). "Something was wrong": A narrative inquiry of becoming a father of a child with an intellectual disability in Ireland. *British Journal of Learning Disabilities, 46*(3), 216–224. https://doi.org/10.1111/bld.12230

Marshak, L. E., Lasinsky, E. E., & Williams, C. (2019). Listening to fathers: Personal impacts of raising children with Down syndrome. *Journal of Intellectual Disabilities, 23*(3), 310–326. https://doi.org/10.1177/1744629518801112

Mavrogianni, T., & Lampropoulou, V. (2020). The involvement of fathers with their deaf children. *International Journal of Disability, Development and Education, 67*(1), 45–57. https://doi.org/10.1080/1034912X.2018.1551520

Mazzei, L. A. (2016). Voice without a subject. *Cultural Studies ↔ Critical Methodologies, 16*(2), 151–161. https://doi.org/10.1177/1532708616636893

Mitchell, J., & Lashewicz, B. (2015). More than a pal: The generative leisure work of fathers raising children with autism spectrum disorders. *Fathering, 13*(2), 130–145.

Mitchell, J., & Lashewicz, B. (2018). Quirky kids: Fathers' stories of embracing diversity and dismantling expectations for normative play with their children with autism spectrum disorder. *Disability & Society, 33*(7), 1120–1137. https://doi.org/10.1080/09687599.2018.1474087

Mitchell, J. L., & Lashewicz, B. (2019). Generative fathering: A framework for enriching understandings of fathers raising children who have disability diagnoses. *Journal of Family Studies, 25*(2), 184–198. https://doi.org/10.1080/13229400.2016.1212727

Mueller, T. G., & Buckley, P. C. (2014a). The odd man out: How fathers navigate the special education system. *Remedial and Special Education, 35*(1), 40–49. https://doi.org/10.1177/0741932513513176

Mueller, T. G., & Buckley, P. C. (2014b). Fathers' experiences with the special education system: The overlooked voice. *Research and Practice for Persons with Severe Disabilities, 39*(2), 119–135. https://doi.org/10.1177/1540796914544548

Pleck, J. H. (2012). Integrating father involvement in parenting research. *Parenting, 12*(2–3), 243–253. https://doi.org/10.1080/15295192.2012.683365

Rivard, M. T., & Mastel-Smith, B. (2014). The lived experience of fathers whose children are diagnosed with a genetic disorder. *Journal of Obstetric, Gynecologic & Neonatal Nursing, 43*(1), 38–49. https://doi.org/10.1111/1552-6909.12268

Scorgie, K., Wilgosh, L., & Sobsey, D. (2004). The experience of transformation in parents of children with disabilities: Theoretical considerations. *Developmental Disabilities Bulletin, 32*(1), 84–110.

Sermijn, J., Loots, G., & Devlieger, P. (2009). Het onderzoeken van verhalen over het zelf: een narratieve, rizomatische benadering. *Kwalon, 14*(3), 17–26.

Singh, S. (2019). I am who I need to be: Reflections on parental identity development from a father of a child with disabilities. *Disability & Society, 34*(5), 837–841. https://doi.org/10.1080/09687599.2019.1589754

Tronto, J. C. (2013). *Caring Democracy: Markets, Equality, and Justice*. NYU Press. http://www.jstor.org/stable/j.ctt9qgfvp

Van Goidsenhoven, L., & De Schauwer, E. (2020). Listening beyond words: Swinging together. *Scandinavian Journal of Disability Research, 22*(1), 330–339. https://doi.org/10.16993/sjdr.756

Vandenbussche, H., Van Hove, G., Claes, C., & De Schauwer, E. (2024). Exploring belonging in the documentary inclusief [inclusive] as a matter of care. *Disability & Society, 39*(8), 2172–2192. https://doi.org/10.1080/09687599.2024.2368566

Wright, A., Crettenden, A., & Skinner, N. (2016). Dads care too! Participation in paid employment and experiences of workplace flexibility for Australian fathers caring for children and young adults with disabilities. *Community, Work & Family, 19*(3), 340–361. https://doi.org/10.1080/13668803.2015.1052041

Wright, K. (2014). Becoming-with. *Environmental Humanities, 5*(1), 277–281. https://doi.org/10.1215/22011919-3615514

Yoong, A., & Koritsas, S. (2012). The impact of caring for adults with intellectual disability on the quality of life of parents. *Journal of Intellectual Disability Research, 56*(6), 609–619. https://doi.org/10.1111/j.1365-2788.2011.01501.x

6

Some Final Thoughts

Abstract This final chapter summarizes the key findings of this book. We draw on the work of Davies, Rix, and Robb (*Disability Studies Quarterly, 43*(3), 2024) to ensure that we do not frame this conclusion in a vacuum, but in the context of Disability Studies (in education).

The shared findings between this booklet and Davies et al. suggest a pedagogical-relational perspective on fathering that highlights the transformative potential of engaged and responsive fathering. This perspective provides a robust framework for understanding and supporting fathers of children with disabilities. Finally, in this chapter, we also attempt—without wishing to be prescriptive or exhaustive—to offer advice for practice, policy, representation, and research.

Keywords Final thoughts • Pedagogical-relational perspective • To empower children • Practice • Research • Representation

G. Van Hove, *Fathering Children with Disabilities*,
https://doi.org/10.1007/978-3-031-82960-4_6

6.1 Some Conclusions

At the end of this book—however small it may be—it is good to draw a few final thoughts.

For these conclusions we rely on the article by Davies et al. (2024) to provide some structure. Both Robb and Davies have published on fatherhood and the roles men can play and Rix is a Disability Studies researcher. Furthermore, in their list of key words (Davies et al., p. 1), they use the concept of 'disabled children' without falling into a medical model-driven categorization of labels. They also put 'caregiving' at the center of their keywords. Both these choices closely follow our Chap. 5 (?) of this booklet.

Already in our Preface, we noted that sociological research suggests that fathers are becoming more involved (though certainly still insufficiently) in caring for and bringing up their children. Similarly, Davies et al. (2024, 1) point out that '… there has been an increased focus on the role of fathers in the intimate care of children, as well as on the nature of fathers' diverse and changing relationships with their children…'.

It is also good to read that Davies and colleagues encourage us to take fathering research seriously, and to stop seeing it as a coincidence or as an indirect effect of another research question. Choosing this route means above all (and we have tried to interpret this in detail in Chap. 5) that the fathers' 'experiences' and 'relationships' with their children become central. This inevitably leads to extra attention being paid to the personal meaning that fathers give to these experiences and relationships, and to the personal fulfilment that this brings for them (Davies et al., p. 3).

Some important historical figures are said to have fathered children with disabilities. For example, Albert Einstein is said to have had a son (Eduard) diagnosed with schizophrenia, and Charles Darwin lost his favorite daughter Annie at the age of 10 to TB or a genetic disease.

We included Charles de Gaulle and John Dewey. We hoped to learn something from history by including these famous fathers. The story of De Gaulle allows us to reflect on whether he might have used his powerful political position to put the issue of 'disability' on the political agenda. The story of Dewey, on the other hand, offers us the opportunity to examine whether his pedagogical theorizing was shaped by his everyday life with Sabino. Twice, a child's presence seems not to have provoked major public action. Both de Gaulle and Dewey were intimately involved in everyday parenting but kept it entirely private. These stories show that it is not possible for everyone to leave the private sphere to become activists for a better position for their children.

We are still very much of the opinion that our short chapter on father-artists was one not to be missed. What we see Dan Habib (see Chap. 4) do, for example, can be described as extraordinary. The way Gusti takes us through his book's drawings and stories, showing how he was able to transform his initial fears and prejudices into understanding and acceptance of his son, can help other fathers. It also responds to the call by Davies et al. (2024, p. 2) to take seriously the relationship between fathers and children in everyday situations. It is fascinating to become aware through Gusti's story of the great diversity of fathering stories.

The way in which Pierre Mertens has scanned, analyzed, and developed the care system in a more parent- and family-focused way is unprecedented. If there were to be a Nobel Prize for Health Care, Pierre would certainly stand a good chance of winning.

It's impressive to see how Michael Bérubé, and especially Dan Habib, go even further and work to include and empower their sons. They have become public figures and activists, going far beyond the discussion of everyday parenting. Habib and Bérubé bring the dynamism of their role as fathers to a long-term project (they let their sons participate in the direction/content of new books and documentaries when the children are older) that makes them role models for other fathers who are looking for ways to use their fatherhood to fight for more self-determination, inclusion, and rights for their children. Personal stories and experiences thus become the motor for change. With their artistic products, these four fathers are also helping to transform old images of fathers and to co-create a more active position of fathers. The 'caring masculinity' of our Chap. 5 is represented here in drawings, images, words, and actions. Very personal stories are being transformed into works of art and are thus becoming a driving force and part of a wider social consciousness.

Davies et al. (2024, pp. 2–3) also began to look at reviews to try and find themes in the fathering literature that are beginning to emerge more and more. Our colleagues took a more rigorous approach than we did: they only looked at reviews and excluded literature that focused only on 'coping' and 'stress responses'.

Nevertheless, there are many parallels between their reviewed studies and the ones we were focusing upon.

- It is striking that some of the review studies are limited to fathers of very specific 'diagnostic groups' (children with autism, children with intellectual disabilities). This shows that both Davies et al. and we still see the strong influence of medical model thinking on family studies.
- It is therefore striking that the themes that Davies et al. identify—emotional effects, mental health and coping, support systems, hopes and anxieties—are largely consistent with negative views (burden) of the effects of the child with disability on the parent. These are also findings that fit a deficit/psycho-pathological perspective: a family with a child with a disability is a disabled family; a father in such a family is a burdened father.

It should be clear that this is not the way forward, nor is it our recommendation for further research with fathers. We stick to Lalvani and Polvere's warning (2013). Dominant discourse on families of children with disabilities, based on assumptions of grief, tragedy, and unmitigated hardship, are strongly influenced by the medical model, which constructs disability as a deficit and as predominantly burdensome for both individuals and families.

In view of the brotherhood/sisterhood spirit that we feel toward the article by Davies et al. (2024), it is particularly interesting to test our findings in detail against the findings that they present at the end of their article.

We outline, and link to our own research, the five themes that are put forward.

Most dads, including those in our study, experience a great deal of confusion (2024, 6) when a child with a disability has been born and are unsure of how to respond. Becoming a father is therefore a nice way of describing what often happens: by entering undiscovered territory (see Van Hove et al., 2009), fathers become stronger and start to see their child differently.

Despite the clear research evidence (see also our foreword) that women take on far more domestic and parenting responsibilities, Davies et al.

also find ample evidence that fathers of children with disabilities are also able to re-prioritize (2024, 6–7). In our own research, too, we have come across fathers who have been able to let go of their focus on work and career and look for new priorities that are linked to the needs of their child. As we said, fathers feel a strong sense of response-ability. That this shift in focus is not a piece of cake, we also heard from fathers who had to exchange their 'masculine embodied habitus', practiced in sport and play, for caring and sensitive parenting. Many fathers discover that caring activities provide a meaningful connection with their children (Davies et al., 2024, 8).

Remember the word 'together' used frequently by fathers in our long interviews. The importance of 'relational aspects of caregiving' for some fathers is also noted by Davies et al. (2024, 8–9) in their review. Like our fathers who want to be 'good fathers', Davies et al. see fathers embarking on a journey that takes caregiving beyond the physical. Fathers are in search of information; fathers also work with their children toward greater independence. There is a lot of focus on trying to find a good place 'in the world' for their children. Sometimes this is called 'working toward integration': Fathers prepare their children, but also become their children's advocates to adapt environments.

As in our own research, Davies et al. (2024, 9–10) also find that some fathers are very talented at the discovery of their children's strengths. In doing so, they help others to learn to see the children as unique individuals and not just as part of some kind of clinical-diagnostic group. Of course, this positive image does not take away from the fact that fathers are also worried about the future of their children. In many countries (including rich ones), parents find that asserting their children's rights is often no easy task. So many do not dream naively about their children's future. Our society still has a long way to go.

As their fifth and final theme, Davies and her colleagues (20–24, 10–11) raise the issue of connectedness. It may be clear—and our own interviews showed this—that fathers who care for their children also get a lot back from these children: For example, some learn to enjoy small things, some are taken to places and situations they would never otherwise experience, some fathers say that they have become a better person because of their child.

These five different themes that we found in both our own research and in the review article by Davies et al. could be a solid basis for a better understanding and possibly support of fathers with children with disabilities.

A pedagogical-relational perspective is emerging.

6.2 The 'Final Touch'?

Finally, we briefly discuss the possible implications of our findings for practice, policy, representation, and research, as requested by reviewers of earlier versions of this book.

Concerning **practice**: Our findings should encourage care professionals to actively support the ideas put forward by second wave feminists: to invite fathers to talk about their children in schools and care centers; to no longer focus only on mothers when schools and the care sector seek alliances with 'the family'. According to Pierre Mertens, '*professionals need to work with parents in such a way that they are given the opportunity to "say it all". It is then up to the professionals to select what is relevant for their field and what is not*' (2024, p. 110). It is also good to get to know and appreciate the talents of fathers. The same Pierre Mertens (father-artist) is very sensitive to aesthetics. This is why he was horrified to discover that the little pump in his daughter's head was far too visible. We'll let him speak for himself: '*…The neurosurgeon doesn't think about aesthetics. Not even when it comes to an 11-year-old blonde girl with curly hair. You should be in the operating theatre as a parent (father) to prevent things like this….*' (2024, p. 129).

Concerning **policy**: The EU has recently taken several measures to help male workers who are fathers or carers to achieve a better work-life balance. These measures respect the role of caring fathers. Following rules and advices of the EU, every employee, in Belgium, for example, regardless of the working regime in which he is employed (full-time or part-time), is entitled, for births taking place from 1 January 2023 onward, to be absent from work for twenty days in the period of four months from the day of birth on account of the birth of a child whose parentage is established along his side. During the first three days of birth leave, the employee retains his/her full salary at the expense of his/her employer. It is clear that if fathers feel supported and respected by policymakers, it will be somewhat easier for them to take on their role as fathers.

Concerning **representation**: As long as fathers are not to be seen, or are only to be seen in stigmatizing roles in films, we will continue to be deprived of 'other' representations. Recent examples of fathers being seen in roles closer to the basic ideas of this book are (finally) emerging.

Israeli filmmaker Nir Bergman's film 'Here we are' follows Aharon, a divorced man in his fifties. He has given up work to devote himself entirely to caring for his autistic son Uri. The film reveals that father and son are a good match and have a particularly close relationship. Now that their son has grown up, Aharon's ex-wife thinks that it is time for Uri to move into a group home so that he can learn to live a more independent life. Aharon decides not to go through with this placement and takes his son on a journey across Israel.

The film shows the chaos that ensues when Aharon does not seem to accept that it is 'normal' for children to leave their homes. This film is interesting because the director manages to credibly transform the archetype of the 'symbiotic—(too) close' relationship between a mother and a child with disabilities into a father–child relationship. In this film, the inability to make fundamental decisions, because emotions are getting in the way, is for once attributed to the father. In this sense, the film is a successful example of 'a different representation' of fathers who are responsible for bringing up their disabled child.

Christina Vandekerckhove's film 'Milano' shows us a father who is trying to bring up his deaf son. In Milano—the first Flemish film with a deaf character and a deaf actor—we see a father, Alain, raising his deaf son, Milano, on his own, wanting to give him a better life than he himself ever had. Despite his best intentions, his powerlessness and his failure become apparent. At first, Alain seems like a clichéd deadbeat dad, but his actions and intentions change that image. You feel his helplessness and his will to do better.

Milano is the story of a deaf, but mostly lonely, boy. But Milano is also the portrait of a father: a man in a constant battle with himself (and the demons of his own childhood). More and more, the viewers come to see the wounds that are hidden behind the father's stoic façade, and we understand how hard this man is trying to do his best to spare his son the same pain. How caring he is, in his own, sometimes clumsy, way. But also, how he sometimes stumbles. By trial and error: this is the way in which Alain brings up his son.

Because disability is only part of the puzzle, this film about a father with a disabled son is interesting. It is an example of the use of an 'intersectional perspective' where generational trauma, poverty, drug use, etc., are also present. In this way, the complexity of life becomes more important than 'just' disability as the all-important factor.

Concerning **research**: Researchers can also make a big difference. They can explicitly ask for the perspectives of both the mothers and the fathers. They can actively invite the fathers to take part in the interviews, instead of sending a single copy of a questionnaire to a family address (where we know that it is mainly mothers who provides the family perspective).

References

Davies, A., Rix, J., & Robb, M. (2024). Fathers' relationships with their disabled children: A literature review. *Disability Studies Quarterly, 43*(3), 10.18061/dsq.v43i3.8744.

Lalvani, P., & Polvere, L. (2013). Historical perspectives on studying families of children with disabilities: A case for critical research. *Disability Studies Quarterly, 33*(3), 10.18061/dsq.v33i3.3209.

Mertens, P. (2024). *Liesje. Zoeken naar woorden voor de geboorte en de dood van een bijzonder kind (Liesje. A search for words to mark the birth and death of a very special child)* (New ed.). Pelckmans.

Van Hove, G., De Schauwer, E., Mortier, K., & Bosteels, S. (2009). Working with mothers and fathers of children with disabilities: Metaphors used by parents in a continuing dialogue. *European Early Childhood Education Research Journal, 17*(2), 187–201. https://doi.org/10.1080/13502930902951379

Index[1]

[1] Note: Page numbers followed by 'n' refer to notes.

G. Van Hove, *Fathering Children with Disabilities*,
https://doi.org/10.1007/978-3-031-82960-4_6

GPSR Compliance
The European Union's (EU) General Product Safety Regulation (GPSR) is a set of rules that requires consumer products to be safe and our obligations to ensure this.

If you have any concerns about our products, you can contact us on

ProductSafety@springernature.com

In case Publisher is established outside the EU, the EU authorized representative is:

Springer Nature Customer Service Center GmbH
Europaplatz 3
69115 Heidelberg, Germany

www.ingramcontent.com/pod-product-compliance
Lightning Source LLC
Chambersburg PA
CBHW051931310326
42180CB00004B/219
* 9 7 8 3 0 3 1 8 2 8 5 4 6 *